Healthy
& delicious
muffins

Published by
Hyndman Publishing
PO Box 5017, Dunedin

ISBN 1-877168-45-9

TEXT
© Simon & Alison Holst

PHOTOGRAPHS
© Hyndman Publishing

DESIGNER
Dileva Design

PHOTOGRAPHY
Lindsay Keats

PROPS
Jania Bates

HOME ECONOMISTS
Simon & Alison Holst

PRINTING
Tablet Colour Print

The recipes in this book have been carefully tested by the authors. The publisher and the authors have made every effort to ensure that the instructions are accurate and safe, but they cannot accept liability for any resulting injury or loss or damage to property whether direct or consequential.

Because ovens and microwave ovens vary so much, you should take the cooking times suggested in recipes as guides only. The first time you make a recipe, check it at intervals to make sure it is not cooking faster, or more slowly than expected.

Always follow the detailed instructions given by manufacturers of your appliances and equipment, rather then the more general instructions given in these recipes.

ACKNOWLEDGEMENTS

We would like to thank the following firms who provided us with the following foods and products:

New Zealand Dairy Foods Ltd. for their range of low fat products:
- Anchor Lite Blue Milk (98.5% Fat Free)
- Anchor Trim Milk (99.5% Fat Free)
- Anchor Super Trim Milk (99.9% Fat Free)
- Anchor Calci-Xtra Milk (99.9% Fat Free)
- De Winkel Low Fat Acidophilus Plain Yoghurt (98% Fat Free)
- Country Goodness 98% Fat Free Sour Cream
- Country Goodness Light Cottage Cheese
- Anchor Lite reduced fat dairy spread (with 25% less fat than butter)

S C Johnson & Son Pty Ltd.

for Chef Mate Canola Oil non-stick spray

Alison's Choice for high quality dried fruit, fruit mixtures, candied fruit, nuts, seeds, cornmeal, brans, lecithin, sun-dried tomatoes, and chocolate chips and morsels, which were used in all recipe development and photographs.

Bennicks Poultry Farm, Buller Road, Levin for fresh barn eggs

Goulburn Valley for fruit and puréed fruit in foil-topped pots

William Aitken for Lupi Olive Oil

The following Wellington firms kindly supplied the beautiful tableware photographed:

Theme the green napkin and all china (page 9), the knife (page 40), the napkin and knife (page 45), and the plate (page 57)
Moore Wilsons the bowl (page 21), all china, coffee plunger, shaker (page 29), mugs and all china (page 33).

Contents

What is a
Healthy Muffin?

Chances are, everybody has slightly different ideas about this! Most muffins are lower in fat and sugar than popular cakes and biscuits, anyway! They are also easier to make, extremely versatile, and are enormously popular.

Fat, particularly saturated fat, is a concern to many people, however. Bearing this in mind, and remembering the importance of calcium in milk products, we used the Anchor range of low-fat milks photographed below instead of full cream milk, when making our "Healthy and Delicious Muffins" and found that we got excellent results with all the low fat milks. So, whichever of these milks is your favourite, you can use it with confidence when making your healthy muffins, too!

We have used no butter in the muffins in this book. In its place we have used oil, low-fat unsweetened yoghurt, low-fat cottage cheese and the 98% fat free sour cream photographed below, often in combination with vegetable or fruit purées. These gave our muffins the moistness and tenderness and good flavour required, and somewhat to our surprise, often produced muffins which stayed fresh for several days.

While we have tried to keep the fat content of these muffins down, we do feel that a little improves most muffin recipes. We have used canola oil in our sweet muffins and have given the option of olive or canola in savoury muffins. These oils contain a relatively high proportion of mono-unsaturated fats (see pages 6 and 7).

Low-fat muffins stick to their baking pans even more than regular muffins. Instead of oiling or buttering our muffin pans, we use Chef Mate Canola Oil non-stick spray which works much more effectively and efficiently, so you use only a fraction of the oil you would otherwise.

We have used fruit – fresh, puréed, raw and dried – in many of these muffins. It has added flavour, sweetness, moistness and an interesting texture. We have also used vegetables in our savoury muffins, and made delicious, spicy, sweet pumpkin muffins as well. Perhaps our vegetable muffins may persuade "picky" children that vegetables can taste really good!

Nuts and seeds add an interesting flavour and texture to many of our muffins. These are rich in potentially beneficial oils and fibre, and are concentrated sources of valuable nutrients. Don't hesitate to add extra chopped nuts to muffin recipes if you have and like them, even if they are not listed as ingredients.

We have used wholemeal flour in some but not all of our muffins. If your family hardly notice it, you may like to replace half the white flour in other recipes with more wholemeal. Add a little extra liquid as well, as suggested on page 59. Wholemeal flour contains more fibre, vitamins and minerals than white flour. (If you are replacing self-raising flour with wholemeal flour, add 2 teaspoons of baking powder for each cupful.)

High-fibre bran muffins often please some people who do not like bran in other forms!

It now appears that eggs do not raise cholesterol levels of healthy people. One egg divided between twelve regular muffins is very little per muffin anyway, but if you are on a strict low-cholesterol diet, replace one whole egg with two egg whites instead (see page 59).

Making Healthy
and Delicious Muffins

Please take a few minutes to read this page before you make the recipes in this book. To work really efficiently, and to make your reputation as an expert muffin maker, it helps to know all the finer points! Remember though, that these are general instructions, and that there are exceptions to every rule!

Try to measure dry ingredients before wet ones, since this eliminates washing and drying measuring spoons and cups part way through the measuring.

We now usually measure the liquids into a large bowl, and add the dry ingredients to them later. We can then simply dust off the container in which the dry ingredients were combined, without washing it, saving a little extra time and effort!

Combine the dry ingredients in a dry bowl big enough to mix them in. Sifting or sieving them is unnecessary if you toss or whisk them with a dry whisk or fork once they are in the bowl. Mix them well, so they are well combined. This is important, since later mixing should be minimal.

Next, measure and mix all the liquid ingredients together in a large bowl. If you are adding heated ingredients to liquid mixtures, try to cool them so that your final liquid mixture is not warm. If it is, your muffins may rise in the bowl rather than in the oven. Sometimes it is easier to mix liquid ingredients in a food processor. When we do this, we tip the processed liquids into the dry ingredients in a large bowl. Follow the recipe instructions.

Nuts are a good addition to healthy muffins. You can always add ¼–½ cup of chopped nuts without altering the recipe in other ways. Add chopped walnuts to liquid ingredients so unmixed flour does not stick in their crannies.

Add sugar to dry ingredients, because it makes the dry ingredients easier to fold into the wet ingredients.

The way you combine the dry and wet mixtures is vital. Always tip ALL the dry ingredients into the wet ones (or vice versa) at once. FOLD THEM TOGETHER WITH AS LITTLE MIXING AS POSSIBLE. NEVER use a whisk at this stage. A flexible straight-bladed stirrer/spreader does by far the best job. (See mail order details on the last page.) Slowly bring your stirrer, scraper, fork or spoon down the side of the bowl and under the mixture, then up through it, turning bowl and repeating this until no pockets of flour are left. Stop while the mixture looks rough and lumpy. NEVER give it a quick beat or stir for good measure!

Occasionally a muffin mixture may seem too dry, since ingredients sometimes vary in wetness. With experience, you can notice dryness before you finish mixing. Add 1–2 tablespoons of milk, juice or water straight away, folding it in as little as necessary.

Muffins, especially the low-fat variety, can stick like crazy! Use pans with a non-stick finish, clean these well, and always use a light, even coating of non-stick spray as well. Chef Mate Canola does a great job.

Spoon muffins into prepared pans, helping the mixture off with another spoon. Try to divide the mixture evenly – put as few spoonfuls in each pan as possible. Do not smooth or interfere with its surface. Add toppings (page 60) to any muffins, for extra interest, if you like.

Bake muffins until the centres spring back when pressed. If this is hard to judge, push a skewer into the centre. When it comes out clean, the muffins are ready. Cooking times are only a guide. Ovens vary in temperature. If your muffins are too pale when cooked, raise the temperature 10 degrees next time. If they are too dark, lower the temperature next time.

Let cooked muffins stand in their pans for 3–4 minutes. Like magic, they stop sticking in this time! As soon as the muffin will turn freely, lift it out, and let it finish cooling on a rack. Very small rubber scrapers help remove muffins from pans too.

Most muffins are best served warm. They will stay warm for some time, without going soggy, in a napkin-lined basket or may be reheated in a microwave oven, or in a paper bag at about 150°C in a conventional oven.

Low-fat muffins dry out faster than richer ones. To retard this, put them in plastic bags as soon as they are cold. Freeze muffins you do not think you will eat within a day or two at this stage, too. When practical, warm thawed muffins before serving them.

Healthy
Eating

We all want to live long and healthy lives! But how? Eating sensibly is certainly a good start. We've all heard it said that "good clean living" and maintaining a "healthy (or rather healthful) diet" are keys to this goal. These sayings appear to be borne out – more and more scientific research is emphasising the importance of eating well.

This is not necessarily surprising, as after all, we are quite literally what we eat! Better still, you don't even have to stop eating everything you like – it is moderation that matters! Small, easy to make changes may result in appreciable health benefits. This is great news for those like us, who believe that "We don't live to be healthy – we live better by being healthy!" With a sensible, varied and balanced diet coupled with regular, moderate exercise we are taking an important step towards good health and wellbeing.

Although there are many different ideas about good nutrition, there is one area of general consensus – we should all try to include plenty of vegetables and fruit in our diet every day. By now we're sure that you are all familiar with the "5-plus a day" message that encourages eating at least five servings of vegetables and fruit per day.

There are many reasons that fruit and vegetables are so good for us. Not only do they add interesting flavours and variety to our diets, they are full of vitamins and minerals (including important antioxidants), are high in complex carbohydrates and fibre, are low in salt, and (generally) low in fat. (While vitamins and minerals can also be supplied in the form of pills or supplements, there is growing evidence that these do not provide the same health benefits as those obtained from natural foods.)

Fat is a nutritional "hot" topic. While debate rages about the relative merits of high– versus low-fat diets, it is widely agreed that mono- and poly-unsaturated fats are better for you than saturated fat. By current standards it also appears that most of us still eat more fat than is recommended, especially saturated fat.

For these reasons we have cut down the amount of fat in these muffin recipes, using smaller amounts of either canola or olive oils (which are rich in mono- and poly-unsaturated fatty acids) and have used reduced fat dairy products.

Low fat muffins can sometimes seem dry but we have overcome this by providing extra moisture in the form of extra liquids and/or by adding fruit or vegetable mixtures (which retain moisture) in the place of fat. This provides the best of both worlds, increasing the amount of fruit (or vegetables) and decreasing the amount of fat. In this way we hope that these muffins will make a worthwhile contribution to a balanced diet and can become "sinless" snacks. Best of all, we think these muffins are just as good as their higher fat cousins!

To gain an overall picture of dietary recommendations, check out the information below (based on the New Zealand Nutrition Guidelines, 1995).

What Should We Eat?

1. Eat a variety of foods from these major food groups every day:

Vegetables and fruits – high in vitamins (including antioxidants) and minerals, and a good source of fibre. Aim for at least 5 servings per day (3 vegetable, 2 fruit).
Breads and cereal foods – high in complex carbohydrates and fibre (especially whole grain products). Aim for at least 6 servings per day.
Milk and milk products – good source of protein and some vitamins and minerals, especially calcium. Aim for at least 2 servings per day, preferably low fat.
Lean meats, chicken, seafood, eggs, nuts or pulses – good sources of protein and some vitamins and minerals, especially iron (particularly lean red meat). Aim for at least 1 serving per day.

2. Prepare meals with minimal added fat (especially saturated fat) and salt.

All fat is rich in energy (9 kilocalories per gram), so excessive intake should be avoided, especially if you are trying to lose weight.

Fat can broadly be divided into two categories: **unsaturated** fats (including both **mono-** and **poly-**unsaturated); and **saturated** fats including **trans-**fats which have a similar effect.

Saturated and trans-fats raise blood cholesterol. Fatty meat and full-cream dairy products are high in saturated fats, as are coconut and palm oil. Trans-fats are found in some meat and dairy products, but also some processed vegetable fats like some margarines (less than 1%) and commercial frying fats.

Mono- and polyunsaturated fats actually tend to lower blood cholesterol (although they do so in different ways). Vegetable oils such as grapeseed, corn and safflower are rich in polyunsaturated fats. Olive and canola oil are particularly good sources of monounsaturated fats (which is why we have used them in this book, in preference to other vegetable oils).

Nuts (although high in energy) and seeds are good sources of mono- and polyunsaturated fats, especially Omega-3 fatty acids which may be protective against heart disease (as well as a good source of other vitamins and minerals). Some studies have indicated that eating a handful of nuts (30g) a day may help protect against heart (and other) disease. They make a delicious and nutritious addition to almost any muffin, so why not keep plenty on hand and add a handful here and there.

Remember, most foods contain mixtures of monounsaturated fats, polyunsaturated fats and saturated fats – this means that reducing total fat consumption also tends to reduce saturated fat intake.

Add salt sparingly when cooking – why not try replacing it with other flavourful and interesting ingredients such as herbs and spices.

3. Choose pre-prepared foods, drinks and snacks that are low in fat (especially saturated fats), salt and sugar.

It is easy to control the amount of fat, salt and sugar in foods we cook at home, but foods prepared outside the home, like meals at restaurants, takeaways and even convenience foods from the supermarket (frozen meals, pizzas etc.) can be sources of 'hidden' fat, sugar and salt. Ask for advice on low fat options and/or read the nutritional information on labels when making your selection.

This is particularly true for salt (which can contribute to hypertension). Up to three quarters of the salt we eat comes from processed foods – while we should use salt sparingly when cooking it is far more important to be aware of the amount that may be contained in processed foods. Fresh foods such as vegetables are naturally low in salt so are a good option, or look for low-salt (low-sodium) or reduced-salt labels on processed foods.

4. Maintain a healthy body weight by regular physical activity and healthy eating.

The energy you consume (what you eat), should be balanced with the energy you use (everything you do uses energy, but the more vigorous the activity, the more energy you use). If you are getting more energy than you need from the food you eat (be it from fat, alcohol, protein or carbohydrate) your body will tend to store it as fat.

If you want to lose weight you should try to decrease the amount of energy you are consuming and increase the amount of exercise you are doing. (Remember small, gradual changes are often the most effective.)

The body mass index (BMI) can be used to determine if your weight is in the "healthy" range. To obtain your BMI, divide your weight (in kilograms) by your height (in metres) squared, ie.

$$BMI = \frac{weight\ in\ (kg)}{height\ in\ (m)^2}$$

The healthy range is usually somewhere between 20–29, but depends on age and sex (talk to your doctor or other health professional for more details).

5. Drink plenty of liquids everyday.

Your body loses 1–1.5 litres of water a day, so it needs to be replaced by at least this amount. Some water is obtained from the food we eat, but we should still aim to drink 1–2 litres of water (or other drinks like tea or coffee) per day. You should drink more if it is hot or you are exercising.

6. If drinking alcohol, do so in moderation.

There has been much well publicised debate about the health benefits (or detriments) associated with drinking alcohol. While it now appears that there may be some benefit (or little harm) from a drink or two per day (especially of wine), alcohol should be consumed in moderation. Women should drink no more than 20g of alcohol per day (1–2 glasses of wine), and men no more than 30g per day (2–3 glasses of wine).

Remember too that alcohol is high in energy (containing 7 kilocalories per gram, it is more energy dense than protein or carbohydrate).

Lemon
Yoghurt
MUFFINS

These easy-to-mix, low-fat muffins owe their moist texture to non-fat yoghurt and their lovely flavour to a generous amount of lemon rind. If you don't like grating lemons by hand, chop the rind finely, using a food processor. In fact, if you use great restraint, you can break the usual rules of muffin-making and mix the whole mixture in a food processor.* If your muffins have peaks, you'll know you have mixed too much and can do better next time!

**FOR 12 REGULAR OR
24 MINI-SIZED MUFFINS:**

rind of 1 large or 2 small
    lemons

¾ cup sugar

¼ cup canola oil

1 large egg

½ tsp salt

1 cup De Winkel Plain
    Yoghurt

¼ cup lemon juice

2 cups self-raising flour

Heat oven to 200°C or 190°C fan-bake. Place rack just below middle of oven.

Grate all the rind from the lemon(s) into a large bowl with the next 6 ingredients and mix with a fork or a rotary beater until thoroughly mixed.

Without packing the flour at all, spoon it into the measuring cup and sprinkle it over the mixture in the bowl. Fold everything together until the flour is just mixed in, but do not mix until smooth. (See mixing and baking details on page 5 and/or back cover flap.)

Using two large spoons, put the mixture into the 12 regular or 24 mini-sized muffin pans which have been well sprayed with Chef Mate Canola non-stick spray.

Bake for 10–12 minutes or until the centres spring back when pressed and the muffins are lightly browned.

Leave to stand for 4–5 minutes, then carefully remove from pans and finish cooling on a rack.

Brush warm muffins with Lemon Glaze (page 60) or dust with icing sugar.

Store in a covered container when cold if not eating straight away. Freeze muffins which will not be eaten within two days.

***FOOD PROCESSOR METHOD:** Peel the lemon(s) thinly with a potato peeler and process the rind and sugar in a food processor until the rind is finely chopped. Add the next 5 ingredients and process again until well mixed. Either tip this mixture onto the flour in a large bowl and mix as above OR add the flour to the food processor and process VERY BRIEFLY, in 3–4 one-second bursts, until no dry flour remains. Remove the processor blade and spoon the mixture into the muffin pans. Bake as above. If muffins are peaked, the mixture was overmixed.

Whole Orange MUFFINS

FOR 12 REGULAR OR 24–30 MINI-SIZED MUFFINS:

1 orange (about 200g)

1 cup sugar

1 large egg

½ cup Anchor Super Trim Milk

½ cup canola oil

2 cups self-raising flour

½ tsp baking soda

½ tsp salt

Optional ingredients:
See below

VARIATIONS: *(optional ingredients)

For lower fat muffins, use ¼ cup oil and 2 extra tablespoons of milk.

For fruited muffins, add ¼–½ cup of chopped dates, sultanas or raisins.

Add ¼–½ cup chopped walnuts or pecans.

Before baking, sprinkle with a few pine nuts.

This recipe is a "butterless makeover" of one of our favourite and most popular muffin recipes. If you have a food processor and an orange in your kitchen, we suggest that you make and serve a batch of these, then sit back and wait for the compliments!

Heat oven to 210°C or 200°C fan-bake. Place rack just below middle of oven.

Cut the orange (skin and all) into quarters, then cut each quarter into four or five chunky pieces. Process with the sugar in a food processor, using the metal chopping blade and the pulse button, until the orange is very finely chopped. Add the egg, milk and oil and process briefly until well combined. (Sometimes a few chunks of skin remain unchopped. If necessary, remove and discard these.)

Measure the flour, baking soda and salt into a large mixing bowl. Mix together thoroughly, using a fork. Add any of the optional ingredients* you like and stir in quickly.

Tip the well-blended mixture from the food processor into the dry ingredients and fold together until the dry ingredients are dampened. Do not mix more than absolutely necessary. The mixture should not be smooth. (See mixing and baking details on page 5 and/or back cover flap.)

Coat clean, dry muffin pans evenly with Chef Mate Canola non-stick spray. Using two large spoons, fill the 12 regular or 24–30 mini-sized muffin pans with the mixture, avoiding any extra stirring.

Bake for 12–15 minutes until muffin tops spring back when pressed lightly and a skewer, pushed to the bottom in the centre of the biggest muffin, comes out clean with no sticky mixture near its point.

Stand pans on a cooling rack for 3–4 minutes, then lift muffins carefully from the pans. Store in plastic bags when cool. Freeze muffins not required within 48 hours.

Serve warm or reheated, without any spread.

Crunchy
Lemon
MUFFINS

**FOR 12 REGULAR OR
24 MINI-SIZED MUFFINS:**

2¼ cups self-raising flour

¾ cup sugar

grated rind of 1 large or
    2 smaller lemons

½ cup canola oil

1 cup Anchor Trim Milk

1 large egg

½ tsp salt

¼ cup lemon juice

¼ cup sugar

RECIPE VARIATION: As long as all the muffins are going to be eaten within an hour or so of baking, you can use ¼ cup oil instead of ½ cup. The texture is not as soft, but the muffins are still popular.

Here is the most popular recipe from "Marvellous Muffins", simplified even further and made without butter. This version gets rave reviews, too!

Heat oven to 210°C or 200°C fan-bake. Place rack just below middle of oven.

Measure the flour and sugar into a medium-sized bowl and mix thoroughly with a fork.

Finely grate all the rind from 1 lemon, or most of the rind from both lemons, into another, larger bowl. Add the oil, milk, egg and salt and beat with a fork until well-combined.

Tip the dry ingredients into the liquid mixture all at once and fold everything together until the flour is mixed in, stopping while the mixture still looks rough. Do NOT beat or mix until smooth. (See mixing and baking details on page 5 and/or back cover flap.)

Thoroughly spray 12 regular or 24 mini-sized muffin pans with Chef Mate Canola non-stick spray. Using two large spoons, spoon the mixture into the pans evenly.

Bake for 12–15 minutes until muffins spring back when pressed and have browned lightly. Turn the pans part way through cooking if muffins brown unevenly. While muffins cook, squeeze the lemon juice into a small bowl and measure out the sugar, ready to add it to the juice when the muffins are cooked.

Leave the cooked muffins to stand in their pans for 3–4 minutes, then lift them out carefully onto a cooling rack.

Stir the sugar into the juice, then brush it generously over the top of all the muffins, making sure some of the unmixed sugar is spread on all the muffins. Working fast, brush the rest of the lemon and sugar mixture onto the bottoms and sides of the hot muffins, until all the liquid is used up.

Stand the muffins on the rack until cold, then store in plastic bags in the refrigerator. Without leaving them to become stale, freeze muffins which you do not plan to eat within two days.

METHOD VARIATION: Use the food processor to grate the rind with the sugar and mix the wet ingredients as on page 9, in the food processor method.

See cover picture.

Mango and
Macadamia
MUFFINS

FOR 12 REGULAR-SIZED MUFFINS:

425g can mango slices in light syrup or 1 cup mashed raw mango

1 cup De Winkel Plain Yoghurt

1 large egg

¼ cup canola oil

1 tsp vanilla essence

2 cups self-raising flour

1 cup sugar

½ tsp salt

about ½ cup roasted macadamia nuts*

---

* Macadamia nuts intended for snacking are usually lightly salted. These are fine for use in this recipe.

Puréed, canned mango gives these muffins a delicious fruity flavour, an attractive golden colour, and keeps them wonderfully moist. Macadamia nuts are crunchier than any other nut and contain a very high proportion of monounsaturated oil, giving them a nutritional advantage. Be prepared to buy more macadamia nuts than you need for the recipe. We find these nuts so delicious that it is impossible not to sample them as we chop them!

Heat oven to 210°C or 200°C fan-bake. Place rack just below middle of oven.

Drain the canned mango slices well, mash with a fork on a board, then transfer the mashed mango to a large bowl. Add the yoghurt, egg, oil and vanilla essence and mix with a fork until everything is blended.

Measure the flour, sugar and salt into a medium-sized bowl. Roughly chop the macadamia nuts. Add these to the flour mixture and toss well with a fork. Tip all the dry ingredients into the mango mixture, then fold together until the flour is just moistened. Do not over-mix as this toughens the muffins and causes them to rise in peaks as they bake instead of being gently rounded. (See mixing and baking details on page 5 and/or back cover flap.)

Using two large spoons, place the mixture into 12 regular-sized muffin pans which have been well coated with Chef Mate Canola non-stick spray.

Bake for 15–20 minutes until the muffins are golden brown on top and spring back when pressed in their centres. Leave to stand for 4–5 minutes in their pans, then remove carefully and cool on a rack.

When cold, freeze muffins which will not be eaten within two or three days.

Serve the muffins just as they are, or dust lightly with icing sugar just before serving.

Apricot
and Almond
MUFFINS

FOR 12 REGULAR-SIZED MUFFINS:

425g can apricots in juice

¼ cup De Winkel Plain Yoghurt

¼ cup canola oil

1 large egg

1 tsp vanilla essence

2–3 drops almond essence (optional)

2 cups plain flour

4 tsp baking powder

¾ cup sugar

½ cup (about 60g) sliced almonds*

2 tsp cinnamon

½ tsp salt

* If you can be bothered, toast the sliced almonds in a dry pan until they are just turning golden to really bring out their flavour.

Almond essence is curious stuff! It is very strong and while a little can add a delicious flavour (even when you are actually adding almonds) if you add too much, it tends to take over and dominate everything else. Alison uses it more often than Simon but both agree that these muffins do benefit from a few drops.

Heat oven to 210°C or 200°C for fan-bake. Place rack just below middle of oven.

Tip the apricots and their juice into a food processor and process until well chopped but not completely puréed. Add the yoghurt, oil, egg and essences. Process again to mix well.

Measure the dry ingredients into a large bowl, then toss them together using a fork.

Pour the liquid mixture into the bowl, then gently fold everything together. Mix just enough to moisten all the flour. (See mixing and baking instructions on page 5 and/or back cover flap.)

Spray 12 regular-sized muffin pans with Chef Mate Canola non-stick spray. Using two large spoons, divide the mixture evenly between the pans. Sprinkle muffin tops with a few additional sliced almonds, if you like.

Bake for about 12 minutes or until muffins are golden brown and a skewer inserted into the centre of one of the muffins comes out clean. Remove muffins from the oven and leave to cool in their pans for 2–3 minutes before tipping them out and cooling on a rack.

Serve warm or cool. Store in a sealed plastic bag as soon as the muffins have cooled to prevent them from drying out.

Spicy Peach
MUFFINS

**FOR 12 REGULAR OR
24 MINI-SIZED MUFFINS:**

½ cup sultanas

2x140g pots peaches in
   juice

½ cup canola oil

1 large egg

½ tsp salt

½ cup chopped or crushed
   walnuts (optional)

1 cup self-raising flour

¾ cup wholemeal flour

½ tsp baking soda

½ cup sugar

2 tsp cinnamon

We usually make these muffins using two little 140g pots of peaches in natural fruit juice but at times we replace one or both the pots of peaches with similar little pots of fruit salad. We started buying these little pots for snack foods for children for spur-of-the-moment school holiday picnics but they are such good muffin ingredients that we now make sure that we have them on hand all the time! (Each pot holds a little more than half a cup of fruit pieces and juice.) Make sure that this is one of the first recipes from this book that you try. We find them enormously popular with all age groups, because of their fruit and cinnamon flavours and their soft, moist texture.

Heat oven to 200°C or 190°C fan-bake. Place rack just below middle of oven.

Put the sultanas in a medium-sized bowl, cover with boiling water and leave to stand for 2–3 minutes, then drain. Cool sultanas by covering with cold water for about a minute, drain again and pat fairly dry with a paper towel.

Empty all the contents of the two pots of peaches (fruit and juice) into a fairly large bowl, add the next three ingredients, and beat with a fork. Finely chop the walnuts or put them in a plastic bag and crush them with a rolling pin, then stir them into the fruit mixture. Add the soaked sultanas.

Measure the remaining ingredients into the dried medium-sized bowl, toss well with a fork, then add to the fruit mixture. Fold the dry ingredients into the fruit mixture until there are no pockets or streaks of flour visible. The mixture will look lumpy because of the chunky pieces of fruit. (See mixing and baking details on page 5 and/or back cover flap.)

Using two large spoons, spoon the mixture into 12 regular or 24 mini-sized muffin pans which have been thoroughly coated with Chef Mate Canola non-stick spray.

Bake for 10–12 minutes or until evenly browned and the centres spring back when pressed. Cool for 3–4 minutes before lifting carefully from pans onto a cooling rack. When cold, place in a plastic bag so they will not dry out. Freeze any muffins which you think may not be eaten within two days.

Raspberry
and White Chocolate
MUFFINS

FOR 12 REGULAR-SIZED MUFFINS:

1 cup (150g) frozen raspberries

1 cup (2x150g pots) Country Goodness 98% Fat Free Sour Cream

½ cup Anchor Trim Milk

¼ cup canola oil

1 large egg

1 tsp vanilla essence

2 cups self-raising flour

1 cup sugar

¼ cup white chocolate morsels

½ tsp baking soda

½ tsp salt

These muffins have a really zingy raspberry flavour which goes very nicely with a hint of vanilla provided by a little white chocolate. The chocolate is a case of a little going a long way but if you are really concerned by its presence, it can be omitted. (Try replacing it with the same quantity of chopped macadamia nuts if you want.)

Heat oven to 190°C or 180°C for fan-bake. Place rack just below middle of oven.

Measure the raspberries into a large bowl and leave to soften for a few minutes. Add the sour cream, milk, oil, egg and vanilla to the bowl and stir well so the raspberries break up a little. (The berries don't have to be mashed, but whole berries are quite large.)

Tip the flour, sugar, white chocolate morsels, baking soda and salt into another bowl and stir them together well with a fork.

Sprinkle the dry ingredients into the liquid mixture, then stir until the flour is just moistened. (See mixing and baking details on page 5 and/or back cover flap.) Do not over-mix. The mixture will be quite wet looking but this doesn't seem to matter in the end.

Using two large spoons, spoon the mixture into 12 non-stick regular-sized muffin pans sprayed with Chef Mate Canola non-stick spray.

Bake for 15–18 minutes until golden brown and a skewer inserted into the centre of one of the muffins comes out clean. (The frozen raspberries cool the mixture down, so these muffins do tend to take a little longer to cook.)

Remove the muffins from the oven and leave to cool in their pans for 2–3 minutes before removing and cooling on a rack.

Enjoy warm or cool, then store in a plastic bag. The raspberry flavour actually improves with standing.

Blueberry
Muffin
MAKEOVER

1–1½ cups fresh or frozen blueberries

1 cup self-raising flour

¾ cup wholemeal flour

2 tsp baking powder

1 tsp cinnamon

½ tsp salt

140g pot (½ cup) apple purée

¾ cup sugar

½ cup canola oil

1 large egg

¼ cup Anchor Super Trim Milk

2 tsp castor sugar (optional)

½ tsp cinnamon (optional)

I am often told how popular my original blueberry muffins are. We have found it a real challenge to remove the butter from the original recipe without the loss of flavour and moistness. We solved the problem by adding half a cup of apple purée to keep the muffins soft and moist and to stop them from drying out prematurely. This works so well that it is hard to notice that half the original white flour has been replaced with wholemeal flour. We hope you will really enjoy these "new look" muffins which contain more fruit, some unrefined flour, almost no saturated fat and half the total fat of the original muffins.

Heat oven to 210°C or 200°C fan-bake. Place rack just below middle of oven.

Pick over fresh blueberries, halving large ones, or put measured, frozen berries aside to start thawing. (Frozen berries are best added to muffins when only partly thawed. If completely frozen they slow down the cooking time excessively and if thawed, they stain the batter purple.)

Mix the next five ingredients into a medium-sized bowl and stir them together thoroughly. Put the apple purée and the next four ingredients into a large bowl and beat with a fork to mix well. Tip in the mixture from the other bowl and fold the two together until they are fairly well, but not completely combined. Add the fresh or partly thawed berries and fold through the mixture, taking care not to mix, nor to break up the berries any more than necessary. (See mixing and baking details on page 5 and/or back cover flap.)

Using two large spoons, transfer the mixture into 12 regular-sized muffin pans well sprayed with Chef Mate Canola non-stick spray. (Help the mixture off one spoon with the other one.) This is not a large mixture, so fill the pans no more than ⅔ full. Sprinkle lightly with a topping made by stirring together the castor sugar and the second measure of cinnamon, if desired.

Bake for about 12 minutes if muffins contain fresh berries and for about 15 minutes for muffins with frozen berries. Stand in their pans for 3–5 minutes until they will lift out easily. When cold, place in plastic bags to stop them drying out. Freeze muffins which will not be used within two days.

Fresh

Fruit
MUFFINS

It's nice to know how to put to good use a handful of blackberries picked from the wayside or something from the fruitbowl that is past its best for eating raw. These muffins made by using one cup of prepared fruit (single fruit or a mixture) are popular served warm at any time of the day, especially at the weekend. If you don't have quite enough fresh fruit, just make up the cupful using drained fruit from a small pot or can or berries from the freezer.

FOR 12 REGULAR-SIZED MUFFINS OR 24 MINI-MUFFINS:

1 cup ripe raw fruit cut in 5mm cubes

    or 1½ cups blackberries, raspberries or blueberries

1 large egg

¼ cup canola oil

finely grated rind of 1 orange

½ cup De Winkel Plain Yoghurt

½ cup (140g pot) Country Goodness 98% Fat Free Sour Cream

½ cup fruit juice or Anchor Super Trim Milk

2 cups self-raising flour

1 cup sugar

½ tsp salt

Heat oven to 210°C or 200°C for fan-bake. Place rack just below middle of oven.

Cut ripe, raw fruit into 5–7mm cubes and pack them firmly into a 1 cup measure. If using berries, do not pack them so tightly into the measure that you crush them. Suitable raw fruit includes kiwifruit, feijoas, peaches, apricots, nectarines, mango, bananas, pineapple, pears, blackberries, raspberries, blueberries, chopped strawberries, etc. Do not use grapes, plums or other soft textured fruit, nor under-ripe hard fruit. Make up quantity with other fruit (see above) if necessary. Put prepared fruit aside.

Put the egg and oil into a large bowl. Add the grated rind of an orange, using as much as possible for a good flavour. Add the remaining liquids and mix well with a fork. Add the prepared fruit and stir gently.

Stir together the remaining three ingredients in any suitable container, then sprinkle them over the liquids and fruit. Fold together gently, mixing no more than is needed to dampen the flour. Do not mix until smooth. (See mixing and baking details on page 5 and/or back cover flap.)

Using two large spoons, spoon mixture into muffin pans which have been well coated with Chef Mate Canola non-stick spray.

Bake for 12–15 minutes, until muffins are evenly browned and centres spring back when pressed. Cool for 3–4 minutes before carefully removing from pans. Cool on a rack. Put muffins in plastic bags when cold, freezing those which will not be eaten in two days. Serve warm.

Cinnamon and Apple

MUFFINS

FOR 12 REGULAR-SIZED MUFFINS:

2 medium apples (about 250g each)

1 cup De Winkel Plain Yoghurt

¼ cup canola oil

1 large egg

1 cup sugar

1 cup wholemeal flour

1 cup plain flour

½ cup chopped walnuts

4 tsp baking powder

2 tsp cinnamon

½ tsp salt

Cinnamon and apple are flavours which go wonderfully well together. Although you can use any apples you have on hand, you will get the best flavour when you choose a variety with a 'tangy' flavour such as Granny Smith, Braeburn, Sturmer or Cox's Orange.

Heat oven to 200°C or 190°C for fan-bake. Place rack just below middle of oven.

Grate the unpeeled apples (discarding the cores). Place grated apple, yoghurt, oil and egg in a large bowl and mix well.

Measure all the remaining ingredients into another bowl and stir well with a fork. Add the dry ingredients to the liquid ingredients and gently fold together until the flour is just moistened. Do not overmix. (See page 5 or back cover flap for mixing and baking details.) It doesn't matter if the mixture looks a little marbled. It will look good in the finished muffins.

Spray 12 regular-sized muffin pans with Chef Mate Canola non-stick spray, then using two large spoons to fill the cups, divide the mixture evenly between them.

Bake for 12–15 minutes or until the muffins are golden brown on top and spring back when pressed in their centres.

Leave muffins to cool in their pans for 2–3 minutes, then tip out and cool on a rack. Place cool muffins in a plastic bag, freezing any you do not expect to eat within 48 hours.

ABC
MUFFINS

A is for apple, B is for banana, C is for chocolate! These muffins contain a good proportion of fruit, but children will enjoy them because of the chocolate chips! We usually make these in mini-muffin pans and freeze a number of them because they will thaw quickly in lunch boxes or spur-of-the-moment picnic packs. And it's not only children who enjoy mini-muffins!

FOR 12 REGULAR OR 24 MINI-SIZED MUFFINS:

1 cup (2–3) mashed ripe bananas

½ cup brown sugar

1/4 tsp salt

1/4 cup canola oil

1 large egg

½ cup Anchor Trim Milk

¼–½ cup chocolate chips

1 apple*, grated or finely chopped

2 cups self-raising flour

* Use a "tangy" apple such as Braeburn, Cox's Orange, Sturmer or Granny Smith for best flavour.

Heat oven to 210°C or 200°C fan-bake. Place rack just below middle of oven.

Mash the ripe bananas on a board, using a fork. In a large bowl, mix together the mashed banana, sugar, salt, oil, egg and milk until well mixed. Stir in the chocolate chips and the unpeeled apple which has been coarsely grated or chopped in a food processor.

Stir the flour before measuring, then spoon it into the cup measure without packing it or banging it down. Sprinkle the flour over the top of the other ingredients then fold it in without over-mixing, stopping when there are no streaks or pockets of flour visible. (See mixing and baking details on page 5 and/or back flap.)

Using two large spoons, spoon the mixture into 12 regular or 24 mini-sized muffin pans which have been thoroughly sprayed with Chef Mate Canola non-stick spray.

Bake for 10–12 minutes or until golden brown and the tops spring back when pressed lightly. Leave to stand 2–3 minutes in their pans, then remove carefully and cool on a rack. Store in plastic bags when cold. Freeze muffins which will not be eaten in two days.

OPTIONAL LEMON GLAZE: If you are making these for adults rather than children, mix together 2 tablespoons each of lemon juice and sugar while the muffins cook, and brush the mixture over the hot muffins.

Double Chocolate and
Banana
MUFFINS

**FOR 12 REGULAR OR
24 MINI-SIZED MUFFINS:**

1 cup (2–3) mashed ripe
   bananas

¼–½ cup canola oil

¾ cup Anchor Super Trim
   Milk

1 large egg

1 tsp vanilla

2 cups self-raising flour

2 Tbsp cocoa

½–¾ cup sugar

½ cup chocolate chips

½ tsp salt

¼ tsp baking soda

We make different versions of these muffins, adding extra sugar and extra oil when we feel we want richer muffins which will stay moist for four or five days rather than two or three days. You may like to experiment in the same way, seeing the difference made to the flavour and texture of the muffins when more or less oil or sugar is used. Overripe bananas give the best banana flavour, so don't feel that you should trim off the clear, brown parts from bananas which are past their best eat-raw stage. These will produce a better banana flavour than less ripe bananas.

Heat oven to 210°C or 200°C fan-bake. Place rack just below middle of oven.

Mash the soft ripe bananas on a board or plate, using a fork. Transfer to a large bowl and add the next four ingredients. Stir well with the fork until the egg is thoroughly mixed through everything else.

In another bowl, mix the remaining six (dry) ingredients together with a fork. Fold the dry ingredients into the banana and liquid mixture until all the flour is dampened. Stop mixing while the mixture still looks rough. If you keep mixing until it is smooth, it will be over-mixed and the muffins will be peaked when baked and have a tougher texture. (See mixing and baking details on page 5 and/or back cover flap.)

Using two large spoons, put the mixture into 12 regular or 24 mini-muffin pans coated with Chef Mate Canola non-stick spray.

Bake for 10–15 minutes, until centres spring back when pressed.

Leave for 3–4 minutes, or until the muffins will lift from their baking pans evenly. Cool on a rack, transferring to plastic bags when cold. Freeze muffins which will not be eaten within two days.

Pumpkin
and Pecan 'Pie'
MUFFINS

**FOR 12 REGULAR OR
24 MINI-SIZED MUFFINS:**

1 cup (250g) cooked
  pumpkin, cooled

½ cup Anchor Super Trim
  Milk

¼ cup canola oil

1 large egg

1 tsp vanilla essence

1 cup plain flour

1 cup wholemeal flour

4 tsp baking powder

1 cup lightly packed brown
  sugar

1 tsp cinnamon

½ tsp ground ginger

¼ tsp ground cloves

½ tsp salt

½ cup chopped pecans

The flavourings in these muffins are based on those used in pumpkin pies (which we love). These are such an American classic that we thought we could add another American favourite, pecans. If you don't have pecans on hand (or think they're too expensive), replace them with walnuts or just omit the nuts completely.

Heat oven to 210°C or 200°C for fan-bake. Place rack just below middle of oven.

If you are cooking the pumpkin especially to use in these muffins, the easiest way is to place it (skin-on) in a covered microwave dish (or wrapped in baking paper) and cook on Full (100%) power for about 4 minutes, or until soft when squeezed. Leave to stand until cool, then peel off the skin.

Put the cooled pumpkin, milk, oil, egg and vanilla in a food processor and process until smooth (or mash well with a fork or potato masher).

Measure the plain and wholemeal flours into a large bowl. Add the baking powder, sugar, spices and salt and stir with a fork to combine.

Pour the liquids into the dry ingredients, sprinkle in the chopped pecans, and gently fold together. Mix just enough to moisten the flour. Don't worry if the mixture is not smooth. (See mixing and baking details on page 5 and/or back cover flap.) Using two large spoons, spoon the mixture into 12 regular or 24 mini-sized muffin pans that have been thoroughly sprayed with Chef Mate Canola non-stick spray.

Bake for 12–15 minutes until tops begin to brown and the centres spring back when pressed. (Test to see if a skewer poked into the middle of a muffin comes out clean, if you are unsure.)

Cool in their pans for 2–3 minutes before tipping out and cooling on a rack. Serve warm or cold, freezing any that will not be eaten within 24 hours of baking.

25

Carrot, Apple and Apricot MUFFINS

¼–½ cup finely chopped dried apricots

1 cup (packed) grated carrot

1 cup (packed) grated unpeeled apple

1 large egg

large egg white

¼ cup canola oil

1 tsp vanilla essence

¼ –½ cup chopped walnuts

¾ cup sugar

½ tsp salt

2 cups plain or high grade flour

1 tsp baking soda

1 tsp freshly grated nutmeg

1 tsp cinnamon

These muffins taste really good but their ingredients are hard to guess. Lovely and moist, they may be kept in a covered container in the refrigerator for four or five days although they are unlikely to last this long! To shorten the recipe we tried leaving out various additions but none of our shortcuts tasted as good as our originals, so the recipe remains unchanged! We find that one or two of these muffins, with tea or coffee, make a satisfying lunch.

Heat oven to 200°C or to 190°C fan-bake. Place rack just below middle of oven.

Using scissors, finely chop the dried apricots into a large mixing bowl. Grate the carrot and unpeeled apple with a hand grater, pressing each fairly firmly into the cup. (Use a large carrot and a large apple. A tangy apple, see page 20, gives the best flavour.) Add all to the bowl. Quickly add the egg, egg white and oil and mix well with a fork so the apple does not brown. Stir in the vanilla, chopped walnuts, sugar and salt.

In another bowl, thoroughly stir together the flour, baking soda, nutmeg (freshly grated from a whole nutmeg) and cinnamon. (If you have high grade bread flour handy, use it because it holds all the other ingredients together well.)

Stir the dry ingredients into the large bowl with the liquid mixture and fold together, stopping as soon as no dry flour is visible. (See mixing and baking details on page 5 and/or back cover flap.) Using two large spoons, spoon the mixture into 12 regular-sized muffin pans, well sprayed with Chef Mate Canola non-stick spray.

Bake for 12–15 minutes until a skewer pushed to the bottom of the centre of the biggest muffin comes out clean with no uncooked mixture near its tip. (This will probably be AFTER the centres of the muffins spring back when pressed.)

Leave to stand for 5–10 minutes before lifting carefully from the pans. Refrigerate in a covered container when cold. Warm slightly before serving.

NOTE: This mixture makes somewhat larger muffins, so cups should be filled higher than usual.

Fruit
Medley
MUFFINS

FOR 12-18 REGULAR-SIZED MUFFINS:

1 cup dried fruit medley*

1 cup boiling water

½ cup sliced almonds

1 large egg

¼ cup canola oil

¾ cup sugar

½ tsp salt

¾ cup Anchor Trim Milk

2 cups plain flour

4 tsp baking powder

* Look for this fruit mixture in the Alison's Choice self-select section of larger New World supermarkets. If you cannot get the mixture, chop up a combination of dried apricots, peaches, pears and pineapple.

If you keep wondering how you can get your family to eat more fruit each day, don't forget that dried fruits count too. These muffins have a lovely orchard fruit flavour and an interesting moist texture because they are based on a mixture of dried, cubed fruit. We like to add some slivered almonds to this mixture as well because they add such a satisfying crunch but you can make the muffins with fruit alone, if you like.

First, heat the dried fruit medley and the water together in a microwave-proof bowl on Medium power for 10 minutes, or simmer them on low heat in a small non-stick pan for the same time. Whichever way you heat them, partly cover the fruit (with greaseproof paper or a lid which is ajar) so that nearly all the liquid has been soaked up by the fruit at the end of the cooking time. Stir in the almonds (which will soak up any remaining liquid), then spread the fruit and nuts out thinly on an uncovered, large, flat plate, so they can cool COMPLETELY before they are mixed with anything else.

Meanwhile, heat the oven to 200°C or 190°C fan-bake and coat the muffin pans with Chef Mate Canola non-stick spray.

Put the egg, oil, sugar, salt and milk in a large bowl and stir with a fork until completely mixed. In a smaller bowl, stir the flour and baking powder together. Mix the cold fruit and nuts evenly through the liquid mixture, then tip in the flour mixture. Fold together, taking care not to overmix, stopping when there are no streaks of flour and the mixture looks rough rather than smooth. (See mixing and baking details on page 5 and/or back cover flap.)

Using two large spoons, spoon the mixture into 12-18 regular-sized, prepared muffin pans, so that each is about three-quarters full. You may find that you have more mixture than will fit in 12 muffin cups. If necessary, leave the rest of the mixture to be cooked after the first batch is finished.

Bake for 12–15 minutes, until the centres spring back and a skewer pushed to the bottom comes out without any uncooked mixture near its tip. Leave to stand for 5 minutes before lifting gently from the pans and cooling on a rack. For best flavour, eat cool or cold after dusting with a little icing sugar.

VARIATION: Omit almonds and reserve 2 tablespoons of milk, adding it only if the mixture looks dry.

Moist
Chocolate
MUFFINS

**FOR 12 REGULAR OR
24 MINI-SIZED MUFFINS:**

1 cup (about 200g) moist,
    pitted prunes

½ cup boiling water

½ cup cold water

½ cup (150g) Country
    Goodness 98% Fat Free
    Sour Cream

¼ cup canola oil

1 large egg

1½ tsp lecithin (optional)

1¾ cups plain flour

½ cup sugar

¼ cup cocoa powder

4 tsp baking powder

½ tsp salt

¼ cup chocolate chips
    (optional)

These muffins are so moist and delicious it's hard to believe that they're actually pretty low in fat. If you really want to lower the fat content even further, you can omit the chocolate chips, but, in fact, there is only 1 teaspoonful of them per (regular-sized) muffin. It really is a case of a little going a long way.

Heat oven to 190°C or 180°C fan-bake. Place rack just below middle of oven.

Put the halved prunes in a food processor and add the boiling water. Process until the prunes are well chopped, then add the next 4 (or 5 if using the lecithin) ingredients and process until the mixture is smooth and creamy.

Measure the remaining dry ingredients, including the chocolate chips (if using), into a large bowl and toss together until well mixed.

Pour the liquid ingredients into the dry mixture, and fold together gently, stirring no more than is absolutely necessary. (See page 5 and/or back cover flap for mixing and baking details.)

Using two large spoons, put the mixture into 12 regular or 24 mini-sized muffins pans, sprayed with Chef Mate Canola non-stick spray.

Bake for 12–15 minutes until centres spring back when pressed or a skewer comes out clean. Remember that mini muffins will cook more quickly than larger muffins.

Remove from the oven and leave to cool in the pans for 2–3 minutes until the muffins will come out cleanly. Serve dusted lightly with icing sugar.

NOTE: See page 39 for lecithin details.

Multi-seed
MUFFINS

**FOR 12 REGULAR OR
24 MINI-SIZED MUFFINS:**

1 cup sesame seeds

¼ cup pumpkin seeds

¼ cup sunflower seeds

2 Tbsp poppy seeds

1 cup sugar

rind of 1 orange

½ tsp salt

1 cup flour

4 tsp baking powder

1 large egg

¾ cup Anchor Super Trim
   Milk

¼ cup canola oil

In these muffins we have replaced half of the flour we would normally use with finely ground, lightly toasted sesame seeds. This adds a mild but "warm" and pleasing, nutty flavour as well as extra protein and "good" nut oils to the muffins. Poppy seeds add interesting crunch and colour as do some pumpkin and sunflower seeds. A food processor grinds the seeds almost as fine as wholemeal flour and is an essential prerequisite for this recipe.

Heat the oven to 210°C or 200°C fan-bake. Place rack just below the middle of oven.

Put the sesame seeds in a sponge-roll or other shallow baking pan. Put the pumpkin and sunflower seeds in two other small metal containers, then put all three containers in the oven to lightly roast while the oven is heating. Set a timer for 2 minutes, and check the seeds every time it goes off, resetting it as often as necessary. Remove the pumpkin and sunflower seeds as soon as some of them have browned lightly. Continue heating the sesame seeds until the lightest seeds have turned straw-coloured. Do not let any of the seeds turn dark brown. Cool seeds on a cold surface. Mix the pumpkin, sunflower and poppy seeds but put the sesame seeds aside separately.

Put the sugar and the thinly peeled orange rind (a potato peeler does this well) in a food processor. Process until the peel is finely chopped through the sugar. Add the sesame seeds and process until ground. Add the salt, flour and baking powder and process until well mixed.

Mix the egg, milk and oil together in a large bowl using a fork. Tip everything from the food processor into the bowl, sprinkle in the mixed seeds and fold together, mixing no more than necessary. The mixture should be slightly wetter than most other muffin mixtures. (See mixing and baking details on page 5 and/or back cover flap.) Using two large spoons, spoon mixture into pans which have been well coated with Chef Mate Canola non-stick spray.

Bake for 10–15 minutes, until evenly golden brown, with centres that spring back when pressed. Leave cooked muffins for 5 minutes before taking them from their pans. Put muffins in plastic bags when cold, freezing any which you will not eat within two days.

Strawberries
-n-Cream
MUFFINS

FOR 12 REGULAR-SIZED MUFFINS:

140g pot (½ cup) puréed apple-strawberry (or apple)

1 large egg

150g (½ cup) Country Goodness 98% Fat Free Sour Cream

¼ cup canola oil

½ tsp salt

2 cups self-raising flour

¾ cup sugar

about ¼ cup strawberry jam

Although these muffins may sound as if they are sinfully rich, the cream in question has only two percent fat. We experimented with different ways of putting the jam in the muffins. When we dropped a teaspoonful on top, it sometimes dribbled over the top and down the side as it cooked. When we made a depression in the top with a wet teaspoon and dropped the jam into this hole, the top of the muffin stayed flat and the sides rose in an odd way during cooking. When we put half the muffin mixture into the tray, topped this with a blob of jam, then covered it with the remaining muffin mixture, we got nicely risen muffins with jam hidden in the middle.

Heat oven to 210°C or 200°C fan-bake. Place rack just below middle of oven.

Tip the apple-strawberry (or apple) purée into a large bowl. Add the egg, sour cream, oil and salt and beat with a fork until well-mixed.

In another bowl, stir together the flour and sugar until thoroughly mixed, then sprinkle it over the liquid mixture and fold in, mixing only until there are no streaks of flour visible. Do not over-mix or the muffins will be tough. (See mixing and baking details on page 5 and/or back cover flap.)

Thoroughly spray the 12 regular-sized muffin pans with Chef Mate Canola non-stick spray and spoon in enough batter until each muffin cup is about ⅓ full. Using two teaspoons, drop a (level) spoonful of jam into the centre of each portion of muffin mixture, then spoon the remaining mixture on top. Do not stir or disturb the muffin mixture any more than you really need to, or you will affect the quality of the muffins.

Bake for 12–15 minutes, until the muffins are golden brown and the tops feel fairly firm when pressed. (The hot jam in the centre of each muffin makes the tops feel softer than usual.) These muffins tend to take longer to cook than other muffins the same size.

Leave muffins to stand in their pans for 2–3 minutes, then loosen, taking special care if any jam has oozed onto the muffin pans. Cool muffins on a rack and dust with icing sugar before serving warm for dessert or with afternoon tea or coffee.

NOTE: Take care to "centre" the jam in the muffins, since it sticks to the pans if it oozes out and makes the muffins harder to remove.

Mango
and Orange
MUFFINS

FOR 12 REGULAR-SIZED MUFFINS:

½ cup (65g) finely chopped dried mango slices*

½ cup orange and mango juice (or orange juice)

1 cup De Winkel Plain Yoghurt

¼ cup canola oil

1 large egg

1 tsp vanilla essence

½ tsp salt

2 cups self-raising flour

1 cup sugar

VARIATION: For a stronger orange flavour, add the finely grated rind of 1 orange to the liquid ingredients.

It is nice to find flecks of bright golden, slightly chewy mango through these muffins which have a pleasantly gentle, mango-and-orange background flavour and colour. We enjoy them with coffee at any time of day, finding that a few muffins from the freezer are particularly useful for a quick dessert.

Heat oven to 210°C or 200°C fan-bake. Place rack just below middle of oven.

Using a wet knife or scissors, cut the dried mango slices into thin (about 3mm) strips, then cut these into tiny cubes. Pour the juice over them and microwave at Full (100%) power for 4 minutes, or simmer for 5 minutes. Leave to stand in the remaining juice until cool.

Measure the yoghurt and the next four ingredients into a large bowl. Add the cool mango and its liquid and stir everything together.

Mix the self-raising flour and sugar together in another bowl, then tip into the liquid mixture. Fold together using a flat bladed-stirrer or a rubber scraper, stopping as soon as there are no visible streaks of flour. (See mixing and baking details on page 5 and/or back cover flap.) If the mixture looks too thick when everything is nearly mixed in, add 1–2 extra tablespoons of juice

Using two large spoons, spoon the mixture into 12 regular-sized muffin pans which have been well sprayed with Chef Mate Canola non-stick spray.

Bake for 12–15 minutes until muffins are golden brown and the centres spring back when pressed. Leave in pans for 3–5 minutes, then remove carefully and cool on a rack. Place in plastic bags as soon as muffins are cold.

*We used Alison's Choice self-select dried mango slices, available from larger New World supermarkets. Buy extra and serve just as they are since they make great snacks, especially with macadamia nuts alongside!

Spiced Date
and Walnut
MUFFINS

FOR 12 REGULAR-SIZED MUFFINS:

½ cup chopped dates

½ cup boiling water

½ cup canola oil

½ cup Anchor Trim Milk, or orange juice

1 large egg

1 cup plain flour

1 cup wholemeal flour

½ cup brown sugar, lightly packed

3 tsp baking powder

2 tsp cinnamon

1 tsp ground cardamom

½ tsp salt

½ cup chopped walnuts

A little ground cardamom gives these muffins an interesting 'warm' flavour that's hard to put a finger on. But if you don't have any cardamom on hand, you can leave it out and the muffins will still be delicious.

Heat oven to 200°C or 190°C for fan-bake. Place rack just below middle of oven.

Place the chopped dates in a large bowl and cover with the boiling water. Leave to stand for about 5 minutes, then add the oil, milk (or orange juice) and egg and stir to mix.

Measure all the remaining ingredients into another bowl and toss them together until well mixed.

Add them to the liquid mixture and fold together until just mixed. (See page 5 and/or back cover flap for mixing and baking details.) Using two large spoons, spoon the mixture into 12 regular sized muffin pans, sprayed with Chef Mate Canola non-stick spray.

Bake for 12–15 minutes or until golden brown and the centres spring back when pressed gently and a skewer comes out clean.

Leave to stand for 3–4 minutes or until muffins lift out easily. Cool on a rack, then put into plastic bags, freezing any muffins you're not planning to eat within two days.

Mocha Hazelnut
MUFFINS

The flavours of chocolate, coffee and hazelnuts all blend well in these delicious muffins without any one of them becoming completely dominant. We think these are worth making for the amazing aroma you get when grinding the hazelnuts with the sugar, let alone the flavour of the finished muffins.

FOR 12 REGULAR-SIZED MUFFINS:

½ cup (about 75g) hazelnuts

1 cup lightly packed brown sugar

1 cup plain flour

¾ cup wholemeal flour

4 tsp baking powder

2 Tbsp cocoa powder

½ tsp salt

2 tsp instant coffee

2 Tbsp hot water

1 cup less 2 Tbsp Anchor Super Trim Milk

¼ cup canola oil

1 large egg

1 tsp vanilla essence

Heat oven to 210°C or 200°C for fan-bake. Place rack just below middle of oven.

When the oven is hot (after about 5 minutes) spread the hazelnuts over a tray and place them in the oven for 5 minutes or until they have lightly browned. (Watch them carefully as they can burn quickly and become unpleasant tasting.)

Allow the nuts to cool, then place them in a food processor with the brown sugar. Process until the nuts are evenly and finely chopped through the sugar. (Option: Remove 1–2 tablespoons of the sugar-nut mixture and set it aside to use as a topping.) Add the next 5 ingredients to the processor and whizz until well mixed.

Put the instant coffee in a cup measure, then add the hot water and stir until the coffee has dissolved. Add milk to make up to 1 cup. Pour the coffee-milk mixture into a large bowl, then add the oil, egg and vanilla and mix well.

Sprinkle the dry mixture into the liquid mixture and stir gently until just combined. Do not overmix. (See mixing and baking details on page 5 and/or back cover flap.) This should be quite a wet looking mixture, so don't be alarmed!

Using two large spoons, spoon the batter evenly into 12 regular-sized muffin pans that have been well coated with Chef Mate Canola non-stick spray. If desired, sprinkle the tops with the reserved sugar-nut mixture.

Bake for 15 minutes. Remove from the oven and cool for 2–3 minutes in their pans before tipping out and cooling on a rack.

Enjoy the muffins warm from the oven or cool and store in a sealed plastic bag.

Cranberry
and Apple
MUFFINS

**FOR 12 REGULAR-SIZED
MUFFINS:**

½ cup (60g) dried
    cranberries (sometimes
    called craisins)

½ cup boiling water

140g pot (½ cup) apple
    purée (see recipe)

¼ cup canola oil

1 large egg

¼–½ cup chopped walnuts
    (optional)

1 cup self-raising flour

¾ cup wholemeal flour

¾ cup sugar

2 tsp baking powder

½ tsp salt

VARIATION: For Sultana and
Apple Muffins, replace the
cranberries with sultanas.
Pour boiling water over
them and proceed in the
same way.

A good way to produce tender, moist muffins using the
minimum amount of oil or butter is to add fruit purée to
the uncooked mixture. (We use small 140g pots of
apple purée, available in supermarkets, with great
success.) We have added dried cranberries as well since
we enjoy their tartness but you can replace them with
sultanas or raisins, if you prefer these. The nuts are
optional but add an interesting crunch.

Heat oven to 210°C or 200°C fan-bake. Place rack just below
middle of oven.

In a large bowl, pour the boiling water over the dried
cranberries and leave them to stand for about 5 minutes to
plump up the fruit. Without draining away the remaining
water, add the flavoured or plain purée, the oil and the egg,
and mix well with a fork. Stir in the chopped nuts, if you are
adding them.

Measure the flours into another bowl or suitable container. Take
care not to use more than you should. (Stir the flours in their
original container, then spoon it lightly into the measures,
without any shaking or banging.) Add the remaining dry
ingredients and mix the lot with a fork. (See mixing and
baking details on page 5 and/or back cover flap.) Sprinkle this
mixture over the liquid ingredients and fold them together,
stopping as soon as there are no pockets or streaks of flour.
(Add 1–2 tablespoons of milk if the mixture looks dry when
nearly all the flour has been folded in.)

Using two large spoons, spoon the mixture into 12 regular-
sized muffin pans, well sprayed with Chef Mate Canola non-
stick spray.

Bake for 10–12 minutes, until lightly browned and the centres
spring back when pressed.

Stand in their pans for 2–4 minutes, or until the muffins may
be lifted out without breaking them.

Leave the muffins plain, dust with icing sugar, drizzle with
lemon glaze (page 60) or coat with crunchy lemon topping
(page 60) as soon as you have taken them from their pans.

Serve at any time of day with tea or coffee or
serve with hot or cold sliced ham or
turkey as part of a festive meal.

Date,
Lemon and Yoghurt
MUFFINS

Dates puréed into a smooth mixture add sweetness as well as moistness to these muffins which have a slight lemony tang as well. A food processor makes the preparation of the liquid mixture very easy.

FOR 12-18 REGULAR-SIZED MUFFINS:

rind of 1 lemon

¼ cup sugar

1 cup (150g) dates, halved

½ cup boiling water

juice of 1 lemon made up to ½ cup with cold water

1 large egg

½ cup De Winkel Plain Yoghurt

¼ cup canola oil

½ cup crushed or finely chopped walnuts

½ tsp salt

1 cup self-raising flour

¾ cup wholemeal flour

2 tsp baking powder

Heat oven to 200°C or 190°C fan-bake. Place rack below middle of oven.

Peel the lemon into the food processor bowl. Add the sugar and process to finely chop the peel. Halve the dates (a double check that no stones remain in them), add the boiling water and process to purée them and mix the lemon rind through them.

Squeeze the juice from the lemon, make it up to ½ cup with cold water, add it to the dates and process again. Add the egg, the yoghurt and the oil and process again. Crush the walnuts in a plastic bag, using a rolling pin, and add to the food processor with the salt. Process until the nuts are finely ground.

Stir both the flours with a fork, spoon them lightly into the measuring cups, then mix them and the baking powder thoroughly in a large bowl. Tip in the mixture from the food processor and fold it into the dry ingredients, stirring no more than is absolutely necessary. Do NOT mix until smooth. (See mixing and baking details on page 5 and/or back cover flap.)

Using two large spoons, fill 12–18 regular-sized muffin pans which have been well-sprayed with Chef Mate Canola non-stick spray to about ⅞ full. If all the mixture does not fit into the 12 pans, leave it to stand in a cool place, without stirring it, until the first batch has cooked.

Bake for about 15 minutes until the centres spring back when pressed, and a skewer pushed to the bottom of the largest muffin comes out clean, without any uncooked mixture near its tip. Leave to stand for 2–3 minutes, or until the muffins will lift out cleanly. Top with lemon glaze (page 60) if you like.

VARIATION: To make these by hand, grate the lemon rind onto the chopped dates. (Do not add the sugar until the egg is added.) Chop the dates finely and pour the boiling water over them and the lemon rind to soften before mashing the dates. Crush the walnuts completely, using a rolling pin, before adding them to the liquids.

Spiced Prune
MUFFINS

FOR 12-15 REGULAR-SIZED MUFFINS:

1 cup (200g) moist, pitted prunes

½ cup very hot water

½ cup cold water, orange juice or apple juice

1½ tsp lecithin

¼ cup canola oil

½ cup De Winkel Plain Yoghurt

1 large egg

1 tsp vanilla

½ tsp salt

¾ cup wholemeal flour

1 cup plain flour

2 tsp baking powder

½ tsp baking soda

2 tsp cinnamon

2 tsp mixed spice

½ cup brown sugar

¼-½ cup walnuts (optional)

2 tsp castor sugar (optional)

½ tsp cinnamon (optional)

Although these delicious muffins have a long ingredients list, they are easy to make. The prune purée in them is important for several reasons. First and foremost, it tastes good! Next, prunes are especially high in antioxidants and since each muffin contains the equivalent of two prunes, they are "extra-healthy". As well, prune purée is widely used in North America as a fat replacement in baking, so these muffins are as moist and "more-ish" as muffins with a much higher fat content. See for yourself!

Heat oven to 200°C or 190°C for fan-bake. Place rack just below middle of oven.

If measuring the prunes in a cup, pack them fairly firmly. Halve the prunes into a food processor. (This is also a double-check that no stones remain.) Add the almost boiling water and process in bursts until the prunes form a lumpy purée. Add the next 7 ingredients and process until the prune mixture is thick and fairly smooth. (Lecithin is a bread-making ingredient. It is not essential, but it makes the muffins softer and moister. Look for it in bulk in larger New World supermarkets.)

Measure the next 7 ingredients into a large bowl. Add the chopped walnuts if you are using them, then mix everything thoroughly, first with a fork, then with your fingers, making sure there are no lumps.

Tip all the liquid mixture from the food processor into the dry ingredients and fold together both mixtures until all the flour is dampened, taking care not to mix more than necessary. (See mixing and baking details on page 5 and/or on back flap.) Using two large spoons, spoon the mixture evenly into 12-15 regular-sized muffin pans, which have been well sprayed with Chef Mate Canola non-stick spray.

Bake for 12-15 minutes until the centres spring back when pressed and a skewer pushed deeply into the biggest muffin comes out clean.

Cool in the pans for 5 minutes, then lift carefully onto a rack. When cold, store in plastic bags and refrigerate, or freeze muffins which you will not eat within two days.

TOPPING: If you would like a spicy topping on these muffins, mix the castor sugar and cinnamon and sprinkle evenly over the uncooked muffins (see page 60).

Fig
and Honey
MUFFINS

FOR 12 REGULAR-SIZED MUFFINS:

150g dried figs
½ cup boiling water

½ cup honey
1 large egg
¼ cup canola oil
2 tsp cinnamon
½ tsp salt
½ cup De Winkel Plain Yoghurt
¼ – ½ cup chopped almonds

1 cup self-raising flour
¾ cup wholemeal flour
½ tsp baking soda

2 Tbsp lemon juice
2 Tbsp sugar

These muffins are made with ingredients we have enjoyed in Greece – plump, tree-ripened figs splitting in the sun; little bowls of yoghurt drizzled with honey and sprinkled with nuts; and warm pastries flavoured with spices, more honey, and more nuts. As long as you like the feeling of fig seeds in your mouth, we think you will enjoy these as much as we do.

Heat oven to 210°C or 200°C fan-bake. Place rack just below middle of oven.

Put the figs in a microwave-proof jug or bowl, pour on the water, cover and heat on Full (100%) power for 5 minutes. Without draining them, put the figs aside to cool. (This is the most efficient way to cook the figs but you can simmer them in water for about 15 minutes, if you like.)

Measure the honey into a fairly large bowl and warm it just until it is liquid. Add the next five ingredients and beat with a fork until thoroughly mixed. Chop the almonds so they are in fairly chunky pieces and stir them into the liquid honey.

When the figs are cool enough to handle, lift them onto a board, cut off and discard their stem ends, then chop them finely. Put them in a measuring cup and add enough of their cooking liquid to fill the one-cup measure, then stir them into the liquid honey mixture.

Measure the flours and the baking soda into any suitable container, stir with a fork, then sprinkle over the cold liquids. (See mixing and baking details on page 5 and/or back cover flap.) Fold together until no streaks of flour are visible. Using two large spoons, spoon mixture into 12 regular-sized muffin pans which have been thoroughly sprayed with Chef Mate Canola non-stick spray.

Bake for 10–12 minutes, or until the centres spring back when lightly pressed. Leave in the pans for 2–3 minutes while you mix the lemon juice and sugar. Carefully transfer muffins from the pans to a rack. Brush with the lemon mixture, making sure that some of the undissolved sugar is on each muffin.

Serve warm. Place muffins that are not to be eaten straight away in plastic bags. Freeze muffins that will not be eaten within 48 hours.

Sultana and Apple
BRAN MUFFINS

FOR 12 REGULAR-SIZED MUFFINS:

1 cup sultanas

1 large egg
½ cup De Winkel Plain Yoghurt
½ cup canola oil
2 tsp cinnamon
2 tsp mixed spice
½ tsp salt
1 large (tangy) apple

¾ cup brown sugar
1 cup baking bran (wheat bran)
1 cup plain flour
1 tsp baking soda
½ cup walnuts (optional)

Don't worry about their appearance when you take these fruity, moist and delicious muffins from the oven because they are meant to have flat tops! If you think they look better upside down, like little sand castles, just turn them over! Enjoy their flavour and texture, eating them just as they are, without any toppings, for breakfast, in packed lunches, as an after-school snack, or with a cup of coffee.

Heat oven to 200°C or to 190°C fan-bake. Place rack just below middle of oven.

Measure the sultanas into a medium-sized bowl you will later use for the dry ingredients. Pour on enough boiling water to cover them and leave to stand.

Put the egg and the next five ingredients into a large bowl. Beat with a fork to mix, then grate the unpeeled apple and stir it through the liquid mixture, working quickly to stop the apple browning. (An apple which is tart as well as sweet, such as Granny Smith, Cox's Orange, Sturmer or Braeburn, will give you the best flavour.)

Drain the sultanas, cool under running cold water, then pat them dry with a paper towel. Stir them into the apple mixture. Dry the bowl and measure the sugar, bran, flour and baking soda into it. If you are adding the walnuts, chop them roughly, or put them in a plastic bag and break them up with a rolling pin. Either way, leave some fairly big pieces of nuts. Add them to the dry ingredients. Using your fingers, mix all the dry ingredients, making sure that the soda is mixed through everything else and there are no lumps of sugar.

Tip all the dry ingredients at once into the large bowl and fold everything together, mixing just enough to dampen the dry ingredients. Do not stir until smooth. (See mixing and baking details on page 5 and/or back cover flap.) Using two large spoons, put the mixture into 12 regular-sized muffin pans which have been well sprayed with Chef Mate Canola non-stick spray.

Bake for 12–15 minutes or until the tops spring back when pressed in the middle and a skewer pushed deeply into the centre of the biggest muffin comes out clean. Leave in the pan for 3–5 minutes, until they loosen, and you can lift them out carefully without breaking them. Put in a plastic bag when cool. Freeze or eat within two days.

Glazed
Pineapple
BRAN MUFFINS

FOR 24 MINI-SIZED MUFFINS:

1 cup extruded bran cereal
(see recipe)

¾ cup Anchor Trim Milk

1 large egg

½ tsp vanilla

½ tsp salt

225g can (1 cup) crushed
pineapple

¼ cup canola oil

¾ cup (packed) brown
sugar

1½ cups self-raising flour

These little one-bowl muffins are quickly made. They have a light colour and texture, even though the mixture contains a cup of bran breakfast cereal (the extruded type, like little sticks, which we buy in bulk rather than prepackaged). As well as being in a very palatable form, this cereal adds a nice malty flavour. We find these muffins as popular with children as they are with adults, particularly when served warm for a late weekend breakfast.

As soon as you think of making these muffins, pour the bran cereal into a large bowl, add the milk and leave it to stand for at least 10 minutes to soften.

While you wait, heat the oven to 210°C or 200°C fan-bake. Place rack just below the middle of the oven. Get out the remaining ingredients and put aside 2 teaspoons of pineapple juice for the pineapple glaze on page 60.

Add the next five ingredients to the bran mixture and stir well with a fork to mix. (Use the liquid from the can, as well as the pineapple itself.) Stir in the brown sugar and sprinkle on the flour which has been stirred lightly before measuring. (Do not bang the cup or pack the flour down.) Fold in the flour until the mixture is no longer streaked with it, but stir no more than necessary. The mixture will look rougher than normal because of the pieces of pineapple. (See mixing and baking details on page 5 and/or back cover flap.)

Thoroughly coat the 24 mini-sized muffin pans with Chef Mate Canola non-stick spray, then fill them evenly with the mixture, using two large spoons.

Bake the muffins in the preheated oven for 10–12 minutes until lightly browned and they spring back when pressed lightly in the centre. These muffins should lift out of the mini-pans almost straight away. If they don't, leave for about 2 minutes, then try again. Place muffins close together on a cooling rack. Drizzle the thin, runny pineapple glaze (see page 60) over the fairly hot muffins or brush it on with a pastry brush. The whole top need not be covered, but each muffin should have some on top. Serve warm, preferably the day they are made. Put leftovers in a plastic bag and refrigerate up to 2–3 days, warming before eating.

Eggless Bran MUFFINS

Warm from the oven, these plain, old-fashioned muffins make a good, very low-fat weekend breakfast or lunch. We really like their golden syrup flavour and often top each half with a spoonful of low-fat cottage cheese for texture and flavour contrast. Each muffin contains nearly three tablespoons of bran, so is really high in fibre. This muffin mixture contains no egg and no added butter or oil!

FOR 12 LARGE REGULAR-SIZED MUFFINS:

½ cup golden syrup

½ cup boiling water

1 cup Anchor Trim Milk

2 cups baking bran

1 cup plain flour

1 tsp baking powder

1 tsp baking soda

1 tsp salt

VARIATIONS: Before you measure the syrup, pour ½ cup boiling water over ½ cup of small, dark raisins or sultanas. After you have stirred the milk into the syrup, drain the hot water off the raisins, rinse them in cold water to cool them, then add to the syrup mixture.

Add ¼–½ cup chopped walnuts to the bran and flour mixture.

Heat oven to 210°C or 200°C fan-bake. Place rack just below middle of oven.

Pour very hot water over a quarter cup measure before dipping it into the tin of syrup. Empty the syrup into the large bowl, then measure another quarter cup of syrup in the same way. Measure the boiling water into the same measure twice, add it to the syrup in the bowl and stir until syrup is dissolved. Add the milk and stir again. (The mixture will be almost cold if the milk was previously refrigerated.)

Measure the remaining ingredients into another bowl. (If you think that there might be lumps in the baking soda, measure it into the palm of your hand, squash it several times with the back of the measuring spoon, then tip it into the bowl with the other dry ingredients.) Using a fork or your fingers, mix everything together thoroughly.

Spray the 12 regular-sized muffin pans thoroughly with Chef Mate Canola non-stick spray. Tip all the dry ingredients into the cool or cold milk. Preferably using a flat-bladed stirrer or rubber scraper, fold the dry ingredients into the wet mixture until all the bran and flour is dampened. Do not beat the mixture at all nor stir until smooth. (See mixing and baking details on page 5 and/or back cover flap.)

Using two large spoons, drop the muffin mixture into the pans. (Expect more mixture, of a wetter consistency than normal.)

Bake for 12–15 minutes, until the muffins are an attractive brown colour and they spring back when pressed. Because the mixture is fairly wet, the muffin tops may be flatter than usual. Leave muffins to stand in the pans for 3–4 minutes, then carefully transfer to a cooling rack. Put into plastic bags when cold. Freeze any muffins you do not expect to eat within two days.

Kumara and Sunflower
SEED MUFFINS

These muffins are just what you need to turn a warming bowl of soup or a refreshing salad into a welcoming lunch. What's more, as they bake, they fill your kitchen with a wonderful aroma. Lightly toasted sunflower seeds are always a good, nutritious addition to savoury muffins, especially if you are cooking for vegetarians. In this situation, as a double check, read the small print on the soup pack to make sure no unwanted animal products are present.

FOR 12 REGULAR-SIZED MUFFINS:

½ cup sunflower seeds

1 cup chopped, cooked, firmly packed gold-fleshed kumara

1 large egg

¼ cup olive or canola oil

1 packet (about 30g) cream of onion soup mix

1 tsp curry powder

2 Tbsp poppy seeds (optional)

1¼ cups Anchor Super Trim Milk

2–4 Tbsp finely chopped, fresh mixed herbs or parsley

1 cup plain flour

1 cup wholemeal flour

4 tsp baking powder

½ tsp salt

Heat oven to 210°C or 200°C fan-bake. Place rack just below middle of oven.

Spread the sunflower seeds on a shallow metal dish and toast lightly in the oven as it heats. Check and shake dish every minute. Seeds may be cooked after 3 minutes.

Stab 1 large kumara several times, then microwave on Full (100%) power, uncovered, until flesh will "give", checking every minute after 4 minutes. Cool, peel, then pack into a cup measure. Transfer to a large bowl, add the next four ingredients, then stir and mash, leaving a few lumps. (Use a potato masher.) Add the sunflower and poppy seeds, the milk and the fresh herbs and mix well with a fork or flat-bladed stirrer.

Measure the remaining ingredients into another bowl, mix well, then sprinkle over the kumara mixture. Fold everything together, taking care not to over-mix. Stop as soon as no streaks of flour can be seen. (See mixing and baking details on page 5 and/or back cover flap.) Using two large spoons, spoon mixture into 12 regular-sized muffin pans that have been sprayed with Chef Mate Canola non-stick spray.

Bake for 12–15 minutes until tops and sides are golden-brown and until a skewer pushed to the bottom comes out clean. Stand 3–5 minutes before carefully removing muffins from the pans and cooling on a rack. When cool, place in plastic bags, freezing muffins which will not be eaten within 48 hours.

VARIATIONS:

Replace kumara with the same amount of cooked pumpkin.

Replace the curry powder with 1 tablespoon of Thai Sweet Chilli Sauce.

Try using other types of cream soup mixes.

Fresh
Asparagus
MUFFINS

These muffins make a wonderful springtime lunch, alone or with a salad. They are lovely and moist and are given a definite savoury flavour from a relatively small amount of one of our favourite soft cheeses, Creamy Blue. This cheese replaces twice the weight of tasty cheddar in other asparagus muffins.

FOR 12 REGULAR-SIZED MUFFINS:

150–200g (1 bunch) asparagus

½ cup water

½ tsp salt

freshly ground pepper to taste

1 cup De Winkel Plain Yoghurt

¼ cup olive or canola oil

1 large egg

50g creamy blue cheese

1 cup plain flour

¾ cup wholemeal flour

4 tsp baking powder

Heat oven to 210°C or 200°C fan-bake. Place rack just below middle of oven.

Slice the asparagus very thinly into 5mm slices, discarding the cut ends if they are tough. Because bunches of asparagus vary in size, you are best to measure the asparagus after chopping it. You need 1½–2 cups of uncooked, chopped asparagus for this recipe. Put the asparagus, the measured water and the salt and pepper in a small pot, bring to the boil and simmer for 2–3 minutes, until the asparagus is tender but is still bright green. Without draining off the liquid, stand the pot in cold water for 5 minutes or longer while you measure everything else.

Measure the yoghurt and oil into the food processor bowl, add the egg, then the cheese, broken into half a dozen pieces. Process until thoroughly mixed. Drain the cold cooking liquid from the asparagus and make it up to ½ cup with a little water if necessary. Add it to the food processor with the drained, cold asparagus. Process enough to chop the asparagus, more if you like smaller pieces in your muffins.

Stir the flours in their original containers, then spoon them lightly into the measures. Using a fork, mix them thoroughly with the baking powder in a large bowl.

Spray the 12 regular-sized muffin pans with Chef Mate Canola non-stick spray, then pour the asparagus mixture from the food processor onto the flour mixture. Fold mixtures together until no streaks of flour remain. Do not mix any more than absolutely necessary. (See mixing and baking details on page 5 and/or back cover flap.) Work fairly fast since the mixture starts to froth up (especially if it's not completely cold) and you need to get the muffins into the oven quickly.

Using two large spoons, fill the muffin pans with the mixture.

Bake for about 15 minutes, until the muffins have browned and until centres spring back when pressed. Leave to stand in the pans for 5 minutes, then transfer carefully onto a cooling rack.

Serve slightly warm, without spread. Put in plastic bags when cold. Freeze muffins which will not be eaten within 24 hours.

Olive, Pesto and Feta

MUFFINS

FOR 12 REGULAR-SIZED MUFFINS:

2 cups self-raising flour

½ tsp salt

50-100g feta cheese, crumbled or cubed

¼ cup chopped black olives

1 cup De Winkel Plain Yoghurt

¼ cup olive or canola oil

1 large egg

2 Tbsp basil pesto

When we think about savoury muffins, cheese muffins are the first to spring to mind. We decided, with some regret, that our favourite cheddar-cheesy muffins have no place in this book but we feel that this recipe, which uses a relatively small amount of lower-fat feta cheese, does deserve to be included.

Heat oven to 210°C or 200°C for fan-bake. Place rack just below middle of oven.

Measure the flour and salt into a medium-sized bowl. Add the crumbled or cubed feta and chopped olives, then stir until well mixed.

In a large bowl, mix together the yoghurt, oil, egg and pesto until the egg is thoroughly mixed through everything else. Add the dry ingredients, then stir gently until just mixed, stopping as soon as all the flour has been moistened. (See mixing and baking details on page 5 and/or back cover flap.)

Using two large spoons, spoon the mixture into 12 regular-sized muffin pans which have been well sprayed with Chef Mate Canola non-stick spray.

Bake for 12–15 minutes or until the tops are golden brown and the centres are firm when pressed.

Leave to stand for a couple of minutes, then remove from the pans and cool on a wire rack.

Serve warm or bag and freeze any muffins you do not intend to eat within 24 hours.

VARIATION: If you like, omit the feta from the mixture altogether.

Pumpkin,

Parmesan and Pistachio
MUFFINS

The pumpkin gives these muffins a wonderful golden colour which looks great with flecks of green pistachio nuts that also add their delicious flavour and an interesting texture. It may seem unusual to include parmesan cheese in a 'healthy' muffin recipe, but it actually has such a strong flavour that, on a flavour per gram of fat basis, it performs much better than cheddar cheese. Grated parmesan is also very light. A quarter of a cup only weighs about 20 grams.

FOR 12 REGULAR-SIZED MUFFINS:

1 cup (about 250g) cooked pumpkin, cooled

1½ cups De Winkel Plain Yoghurt

¼ cup olive or canola oil

1 large egg

1 cup plain flour

1 cup wholemeal flour

¼–½ cup chopped pistachio nuts*

¼ cup grated parmesan

4 tsp baking powder

½ tsp salt

*   About 100g (1 cup) of 'whole', unshelled pistachios gives 50-60g (about ½ cup) shelled nuts. If you don't want to use pistachios, try pumpkin kernels instead.

Heat oven to 200°C or 190°C for fan bake. Place rack just below middle of oven.

If you are cooking the pumpkin especially to use in these muffins, the easiest way is to place it (skin-on) in a covered microwave dish (or wrapped in baking paper) and cook on Full (100%) power for about 4 minutes or until soft when squeezed. Leave to stand until cool, then peel off the skin.

Put the cooled pumpkin, yoghurt, oil and egg in a food processor and process until smooth.

Measure the plain and wholemeal flours into a large bowl. Add the nuts, parmesan, baking powder and salt and stir with a fork to combine.

Pour the pumpkin mixture into the dry ingredients and gently fold together. Mix just enough to moisten the flour. Don't worry if the mixture is not smooth. (See mixing and baking details on page 5 or back cover flap.) Using two large spoons, spoon the mixture into 12 regular-sized muffin pans that have been thoroughly sprayed with Chef Mate Canola non-stick spray.

Bake for 12–15 minutes until tops begin to brown and the centres spring back when pressed. (A skewer poked into the middle of a muffin should come out clean.)

Cool muffins in their pans for 2–3 minutes before tipping out. Serve warm or cold, freezing any that will not be eaten within 24 hours of baking.

Sun-dried Tomato

Cornmeal and Coriander
MUFFINS

The delicious combination of coriander, cumin and a little chilli gives these muffins a slightly Mexican feel! Sun-dried tomatoes add a more intense flavour and chewier texture than fresh tomatoes. Try these muffins with your favourite Mexican foods or with a salad or soup for an interesting lunch. Cornmeals vary in coarseness, and difference in particle size produces quite different results. We use cornmeal that has a yellow colour and is quite powdery but is not as fine as flour. (It still feels slightly gritty when rubbed between your fingers.)

FOR 12 REGULAR-SIZED MUFFINS:

6 large sun-dried tomato halves (¼ cup when chopped)

½ cup boiling water

1 cup Anchor Trim Milk

¼ cup olive or canola oil

1 Tbsp sugar

1 large egg

1 tsp ground cumin

½ tsp chilli powder, optional

¾ tsp salt

2–4 Tbsp chopped coriander leaves

½ cup fine yellow cornmeal

1½ cups self-raising flour

VARIATION: For a stronger, spicy flavour, replace the ground cumin with 1½ teaspoons each of whole cumin and whole coriander seeds. Grind these finely in a spice grinder, before you add them to the mixture.

Heat oven to 210°C or 200°C fan-bake. Place rack just below middle of oven.

Chop the sun-dried tomatoes finely and put in a large mixing bowl. Pour the water over them, cover the bowl and microwave on Full (100%) power for 3 minutes (or simmer them in a small, covered pot for 5 minutes), then leave to stand for about 5 minutes.

When the tomatoes and any remaining liquid are cool, add the next seven ingredients and mix with a fork until the egg is thoroughly blended with everything else. Stir in the chopped coriander leaves and the cornmeal and mix until there are no lumps of cornmeal.

Measure the self-raising flour without packing it down. Sprinkle it over the wet ingredients in the bowl, then fold it in until no streaks of flour remain, mixing no more than you need to. (See mixing and baking details on page 5 and/or back cover flap.)

Using two large spoons, place mixture into 12 regular-sized muffin pans that have been well coated with Chef Mate Canola non-stick spray.

Bake for about 12 minutes, until muffins have lightly browned and the centres spring back when pressed. Leave to stand in their pans for 5 minutes, then finish cooling on a rack. Serve warm or reheated within two days, freezing any that you do not think will be eaten within this time.

NOTE: We used Alison's Choice self-select cornmeal and sun-dried tomatoes. These are available from larger New World supermarkets.

Broccoli
and Blue Cheese
MUFFINS

**FOR 12 REGULAR OR
24 MINI-SIZED MUFFINS:**

200g broccoli (1 small-
medium head)

1½ cups De Winkel Plain
Yoghurt

¼ cup olive or canola oil

1 large egg

50g creamy blue cheese

2 cups self-raising flour

½ tsp salt

¼ cup Anchor Trim Milk, if
required

Neither the blue cheese nor broccoli flavour of these muffins is too strong. Their very pleasant savoury aroma and taste are certainly popular with all our tasters. The relatively intense flavour of the blue cheese means that a little goes a long way. You would have to use far more cheddar cheese to get the same sort of rich 'cheesy' flavour that 50g of blue cheese gives.

Heat oven to 200°C or 190°C for fan-bake. Place rack just below middle of oven.

The easiest way to cook the broccoli is to separate it into florets, then place it in a microwave-safe container with 1 tablespoon of water, cover, and microwave for about 3 minutes on Full (100%) power until very tender. Alternatively, boil or steam until tender, then drain well.

Place the yoghurt, oil and egg in a food processor and mix well. Add the broccoli and roughly crumble in the blue cheese. Process in short bursts until there are no large pieces of broccoli left. (Try not to purée the broccoli, rather just to chop it finely.)

Measure the flour and salt into a large bowl and toss together with a fork. Pour in the liquid mixture and begin to fold together. If you think the mixture looks too dry, add the extra milk and fold JUST enough to combine. (See mixing and baking details on page 5 and/or back cover flap.)

Spray 12 regular or 24 mini-muffin pans with Chef Mate Canola non-stick spray. Using two large spoons, divide the mixture evenly between the pans.

Bake for 12–15 minutes or until golden brown and centres spring back when pressed.

Remove muffins from the oven and cool in their pans for 2–3 minutes before tipping out. Store cooled muffins in a plastic bag to prevent drying out.

Cottage
Cheese and Chutney
MUFFINS

FOR 12 REGULAR OR 24 MINI-SIZED MUFFINS:

½ cup fruit chutney

¾ cup Anchor Super Trim Milk

1 large egg

¼ cup canola or olive oil

1 cup (250g) Country Goodness Light Cottage Cheese

2 cups self-raising flour

1 cup reduced fat grated tasty cheese

½–¾ tsp salt

¼ tsp chilli powder, optional

Obviously the sweetness and flavour of these muffins will vary a little depending on the chutney you choose. We favour a dark, spicy fruit chutney but have also used a lighter, sweeter, apricot chutney with great success too. Simon likes them a little spicier, so he adds the chilli powder, but this is quite optional.

Turn the oven on to 210°C or 200°C for fan bake. Place rack just below the middle of the oven.

If the chutney is thick with large chunks of fruit, place it in a food processor with the milk, egg and oil and process until well mixed, then add the cottage cheese and process briefly until just mixed. (If the chutney is thinner, without large pieces, measure the first five ingredients into a large bowl and mix well with a fork.)

Measure the flour, grated cheese, salt and chilli powder (if using) into another, smaller, bowl and stir together with a fork or whisk.

Tip the dry ingredients into the wet mixture and gently fold them together until the flour is just moistened. (This can sometimes be a dryish mixture, if you think it looks too dry, add an extra 2 tablespoons of milk and mix just enough to combine. See mixing and baking details on page 5 and/or back cover flap.)

Spoon the mixture into 12 regular or 24 mini-sized muffin pans that have been well sprayed with Chef Mate Canola non-stick spray.

Bake for 12–15 minutes until golden brown and firm when pressed in their centres.

Remove from the oven and leave muffins to cool in their trays for 3–4 minutes before turning out and cooling on a rack.

Serve warm, to accompany soup or salad, or just as a delicious snack.

Spinach
and Feta
MUFFINS

FOR 12 REGULAR-SIZED MUFFINS:

½ cup (100-125g) cooked spinach, chopped*

up to 1 cup Anchor Super Trim Milk

1 cup (250g) Country Goodness Light Cottage Cheese

¼ cup olive or canola oil

1 large egg

50–75g feta, cubed or crumbled

1 cup wholemeal flour

1 cup plain flour

4 tsp baking powder

½–1 tsp salt

* For convenience try using half a 250g block of Wattie's frozen spinach.

It's hard to know what makes the combination of spinach and feta cheese work so well but it does! The green flecks from the spinach make these muffins look really good, too. Feta has a lovely salty flavour and "hitting" little pieces as you eat really gives these muffins a lift. It also has a higher water content than harder cheeses, such as cheddar, so is comparatively low in fat.

Heat oven to 210°C or 200°C for fan-bake. Place rack just below middle of oven.

Lightly squeeze the cooked spinach, reserving the liquid. Make the spinach liquid up to 1 cup with milk, then place the spinach, milk, cottage cheese, oil and egg in a large bowl and mix well. Add the cubed or crumbled cheese and mix lightly.

Measure the flours, baking powder and salt together into another bowl and toss with a fork.

Tip the flour mixture into the liquids, then fold gently together until the flour is just moistened. The mixture does not need to be smooth. (See mixing and baking details on page 5 and/or back cover flap.)

Using two large spoons, spoon the mixture into 12 regular-sized muffin pans sprayed with Chef Mate Canola non-stick spray.

Bake for 15 minutes or until golden brown and a skewer poked into the centre of a muffin comes out clean.

Remove muffins from the oven and leave to cool in their pans for 2–3 minutes before tipping out and cooling on a rack. (These muffins do seem to stick to their pans when first removed from the oven but standing for a few minutes really does help removal.)

Serve warm or store cooled muffins in sealed bags to prevent drying out.

Guacamole
MUFFINS

Enjoy these unusual and very tasty muffins for lunch on a sunny spring day since this is the time of year when avocados are plentiful and reasonably priced. Avocados contain fat, but this is predominantly mono-unsaturated (as are the fats in olives, olive oil, and canola oil) and has nutritional advantages.

FOR 12 REGULAR-SIZED MUFFINS:

¼ cup finely chopped sun-dried tomatoes

½ cup boiling water

1 cup avocado flesh (see method)

2 Tbsp lemon juice

2 Tbsp olive or canola oil

1 cup De Winkel Plain Yoghurt

1 large egg

½ cup chopped spring onions

½ cup chopped coriander leaves

1 Tbsp sugar

1 tsp salt

1 tsp freshly ground cumin seeds

½ tsp minced red chilli

1 cup fine yellow cornmeal*

1 cup plain flour

4 tsp baking powder

* Use cornmeal that's almost as fine as flour, with some grittiness when rubbed between your fingers.

Chop the sun-dried tomatoes finely, pour the boiling water over them, cover and microwave on Full (100%) power for 3 minutes or simmer for 5 minutes, then leave to cool.

Heat oven to 210°C or 200°C fan-bake. Place rack just below middle of oven.

Buy ripe avocados that "give" when pressed. (You will probably need 1–2, depending on their size.) Scoop out the flesh from the avocado halves with a spoon, packing it into a cup measure. Transfer it to a large bowl with the lemon juice and mash with a fork. Add the next nine ingredients. (We use minced red chilli from a jar.)

Press the tomatoes, pouring any remaining liquid into a measure. Make it up to ¼ cup with cold water then add the liquid, tomatoes and cornmeal to the avocado mixture, mixing and mashing to remove any large lumps of avocado. Stir as much as you like at this stage, but do not food process since this may make the mixture too smooth and thin.

Stir the flour and baking powder together until well mixed, then fold into everything else, mixing only until no streaks remain. (See mixing and baking details on page 5 and/or back cover flap.) Using two large spoons, fill 12 regular-sized muffin pans, well sprayed with Chef Mate Canola non-stick spray.

Bake until the centres spring back when pressed, about 12–15 minutes. Leave for 5 minutes before lifting carefully from the pans. Bag when cold and eat within two days.

NOTE: We used Alison's Choice self-select cornmeal and sun-dried tomatoes, available from larger New World supermarkets.

Muffin Sizes –
Mini, Medium or Monster?

You can buy muffin pans of varying sizes. Whatever you buy, make sure it has a good non-stick finish, since many muffin mixtures stick badly!

We usually use regular (or medium) sized muffin pans, see our definitions below, but from time to time it is interesting to have a change and try something different. Children seem to particularly like sweet mini muffins, while savoury mini muffins make great nibbles to serve with drinks, either as they are or halved and used as the base for toppings.

Monster muffins can also be fun, especially if you are serving a savoury muffin as part of a meal (for example, accompanying soup or a salad). If, however, you are watching your waist, we suggest that you avoid them, as at twice the size of a regular muffin it is easy to succumb to temptation and eat too much.

Regular (Medium) Sized Muffins

Most widely used are muffin trays which make twelve medium sized muffins. (The twelve depressions, if filled with water, hold 4 cupfuls altogether.) Most of the recipes in this book will make 12 muffins this size. We spoon about quarter of a cup of mixture into each muffin hole.

You can also buy muffin trays with six holes the size of those above. These fit in some bench-top ovens, and are also handy if you have a little mixture left over, and want to make a few more muffins.

We have recently also experimented with some regular sized, flexible silicon muffin trays. These worked well, although the bottoms and sides of the muffins don't seem to brown in quite the same way.

Mini Muffins

Mini muffin tins are fun! Hardly anyone will refuse one of these little muffins which are less than half the size of those above. (A muffin tray holding 12 mini muffins, if filled with water, holds 1½ cupfuls.) A mixture making 12 medium muffins will make about 24–30 mini muffins. Mini muffins usually need a slightly shorter cooking time – take about two minutes off the time needed for medium muffins.

Mini-muffin trays usually fit in bench-top ovens.

Monster Muffins

Monster muffins (Texan Muffins) come in trays of six. Each muffin is twice the size of a medium muffin. Muffins from these trays always look extra-generous. (The tray of six holds 5 cups of water altogether.) These muffins usually take 2–4 minutes longer to cook than medium muffins.

Gem Irons

If you have gem irons tucked away in a bottom cupboard, by all means try cooking your muffins in them. Heat the irons in the oven as it warms up. Put the hot irons on a heat-resistant surface, spray well with Chef Mate Canola non-stick spray, then drop in the mixture from the side of a dessert spoon. The cooking time will be shorter than for medium muffins.

Paper Cases

Paper cases the size of medium muffin pans are sometimes used for muffins which are to be sold or handled a lot. Some muffin mixtures stick to the paper badly, and the muffins break as they are removed. Paper cases are helpful for microwaved muffins which otherwise stick to their plastic pans.

Modifying Existing Recipes
to Make Healthier Muffins

There may be times when you want to make changes, substitutions or additions to your existing favourite muffin recipes. This might be to suit special dietary requirements, to fit in with your own personal eating pattern, to use the ingredients you have on hand, or to 'dress up' your muffins! We hope that the following guidelines, explanations and suggestions will help you to produce good results.

Wholemeal flour

Although white flour contains more fibre than most people realise, wholemeal flour contains even more. Research shows that most of us would benefit by eating more fibre, so using more wholemeal flour when baking is a step in the right direction. Replacing up to half the regular (white) flour in a muffin recipe with wholemeal will usually make little noticeable difference to the finished muffins. Simply substitute up to half the regular (white) flour with wholemeal flour, or half the white self-raising flour with self-raising wholemeal, adding an extra tablespoon of liquid for each cup of wholemeal used.

Low cholesterol muffins

Replace 1 large egg with the whites of 2 large eggs. Use canola or light olive oil, or an olive oil based spread in place of butter, replacing 50g butter with ¼ cup of oil. (You may want to add a little extra salt when replacing butter with oil.) In many 2 egg muffin recipes you can leave out 1 egg altogether. Add 2–4 Tbsp of extra liquid instead.

Lower fat muffins

Anchor Lite (made from butter and buttermilk) is a product that looks and tastes just like butter, but it contains 25% less fat than butter. We have found that you can use it in place of regular butter in muffin recipes with great success.

Alternatively, the butter or oil content of most muffin recipes can be reduced by half (or even more) by adding an equal volume of plain low-fat yoghurt or fruit purée in its place. The texture will not be exactly the same and the muffins should be eaten the day they are made, for best results.

For further fat reductions use any of Anchor's low-fat milks in place of regular milk, and other reduced fat dairy products, like (Country Goodness 98% Fat-Free Sour Cream) in place of their full fat cousins.

Lower fat cheesy muffins

We bake cheese muffins at a high temperature to get an appetising golden-brown coloured crust and a good flavour. Replace grated cheese with quarter to half as much Parmesan for a definite cheese flavour but less fat. Muffins that contain large amounts of cheddar cheese do not need added butter or oil as well.

Non-dairy muffins

Use soy milk instead of milk, and soy yoghurt in place of yoghurt or sour cream. Replace butter with the same amount of dairy-free margarine or with oil. When using oil replace 50g butter with ¼ cup of oil, and add a little (¼ tsp) salt.

Toppings, Glazes and Icings
For Healthy Muffins

Add interest to your muffins by using interesting toppings and spreads on them. If you usually eat muffins buttered, why not try using low fat cottage cheese, or, more sparingly, low fat cream cheese or any of the spreads below as a healthier alternative.

Toppings For Sweet and Bran Muffins

Before cooking, top with cinnamon sugar or sesame sugar, chopped walnuts, almonds, or cashews, sunflower, pumpkin, poppy or sesame seeds, or (a few!) chocolate chips.

CINNAMON SUGAR. Shake together in a screw-topped jar 2 tablespoons of brown sugar, 2 tablespoons of castor sugar, and 1–2 teaspoons of cinnamon. Sprinkle ½–1 teaspoon over each muffin before baking.

SESAME SUGAR. Grind using a pestle and mortar or a coffee grinder 2 Tbsp toasted sesame seeds. Add 2 Tbsp each brown sugar and white sugar, and a pinch of salt. Mix or grind briefly. Store in an airtight jar in a cool place. Sprinkle about a teaspoonful over any sweet or bran muffin before baking.

ICING SUGAR. The simplest topping for any sweet muffin is a dusting of icing sugar. Place a little icing sugar in a small (preferably fine) sieve and tap it gently while holding over the muffins. A little goes a long way and it tends to add immediate mouth appeal when muffins are tasted.

CRUNCHY LEMON TOPPING. While muffins cook, squeeze ¼ cup lemon juice into a small bowl and measure out ¼ cup sugar (don't add it yet). Remove cooked muffins from the oven and leave them to stand for 3–4 minutes before removing them from their pans. Stir the sugar into the lemon juice (not all the sugar will dissolve), then quickly brush the mixture over all the surfaces of the hot muffins. Stand muffins on a rack until cool.

LEMON GLAZE. Make a thin glaze by mixing 1–2 teaspoons of lemon juice with 2–3 tablespoons of icing sugar. Brush or drizzle onto warm muffins as they cool on a rack.

PINEAPPLE GLAZE. Put ¼ cup icing sugar in a small bowl. Add 1–2 teaspoons of pineapple juice (from the can) and stir until thin and runny. Brush or drizzle onto hot or warm muffins as they cool on a rack. (Lay a piece of plastic over the surface of glaze, in bowl, if not using immediately.)

ICING TO DRIZZLE. Sieve ¼ cup icing sugar, add, to make a smooth, pourable cream, 1–2 tsp of water, lemon or orange juice, etc. For a "generous drizzle", double these quantities. Pour over hot or warm, not cold, muffins.

ORANGE CREAM CHEESE SPREAD. Mix together until creamy, in a bowl or food processor, ½ cup low fat cream cheese, 2 tsp grated orange, mandarin or tangelo rind and about 3 Tbsp icing sugar. Use in place of butter.

NUTTY CREAM SPREAD. Mix together, as above, ½ cup low fat cream cheese, about 3 Tbsp icing sugar, and ½ cup of very finely chopped, lightly roasted almonds, brazil or cashew nuts, or plain (unroasted) walnuts.

Toppings for Savoury Muffins

Before cooking, add a few extra shreds of reduced-fat grated or Parmesan cheese or some toasted sesame seeds, poppy seeds, pumpkin seeds, sunflower seeds, paprika, cayenne and chilli powder. After cooking, split muffins (sometimes from top to bottom, at other times from side to side) and spread with plain or flavoured low-fat cottage cheese, low-fat cream cheese, or quark in place of butter (if you need anything at all!).

Crunchy Lemon Muffins, with Crunchy Lemon Topping and a light dusting of icing sugar.

Measures
for Muffins

If you want consistently good results when you make the muffins in this book, you should be precise and measure the ingredients carefully.

Most recipe ingredients have been measured rather than weighed, and the quantities given in level cup and spoon measures.

A set of "single capacity" measuring cups will enable you to measure all your dry ingredients quickly, easily, and accurately. (It is harder to measure fractions of a cup accurately when you use only a one cup measure.) We use one cup, half cup and quarter cup measures, measuring three quarters of a cup using half and quarter cup measures. Occasionally you may see ⅛ cup measures. These little measures hold 2 (15ml) tablespoons and are useful at times, but are not essential.

All the dry ingredients you measure should fill the measures, but should not be heaped up above the rim.

The only ingredient which is PRESSED into a measure is brown sugar. It should hold its shape like a sand castle when it is turned out of its measure.

Flour measurements are especially important when you are baking muffins. Too much flour will make your muffins dry and stodgy, and too little will make them spread too much. When you measure flour, first stir it with a fork or whisk in its original container. Spoon the stirred flour into your measure and level it off with the edge of a knife. NEVER bang or shake the measure to level off the flour in it, or it will compact again and you will finish up using more flour than intended.

We used to measure liquids in clear, graduated measuring cups, but we now find it more practical to use the same single capacity cups that we use for dry ingredients. You should fill the measuring cup so that it is brimming full. Do NOT try to carry a brimming full cup from one side of your kitchen to the other, or you will spill it, and your measuring will not be accurate.

If you get into the habit of measuring dry ingredients before you measure liquid ingredients, you will not have to wash and dry your measures before you finish measuring. Do not measure dry ingredients in a measure which is wet after measuring liquids or some will remain in the cup and the amount you use will not be large enough.

Because household spoons vary so much in size, we always use a set of metric measuring spoons. One tablespoon holds 15 ml, and 1 teaspoon holds 5 ml. (Australian measuring spoons hold 20ml, not 15ml. If you have Australian measuring spoons, use 3 teaspoon measures instead of the (larger) tablespoon. The Australian measuring teaspoon holds 5 ml, as the New Zealand one does.)

Do not use heaped spoon measures in any of these recipes, since a heaped spoon holds about twice as much as a level spoon. Incorrect amounts of baking powder, baking soda and salt can really spoil your muffins.

The following abbreviations have been used:

cm	centimetre
g	gram
ml	millilitre
°C	degrees Celcius
tsp	teaspoon
Tbsp	tablespoon

The following measures have been used:

1 Tbsp	=	3 tsp
2 Tbsp	=	⅛ cup
4 Tbsp	=	¼ cup
8 Tbsp	=	½ cup
16 Tbsp	=	1 cup

Knives
by Mail Order

For about 20 years Alison has imported her favourite, very sharp, kitchen knives from Switzerland. They keep their edges well, are easy to sharpen, a pleasure to use, and make excellent gifts.

VEGETABLE KNIFE $8.00
Ideal for cutting and peeling vegetables, these knives have a straight edged 85mm blade and black (dishwasher-proof) nylon handle. Each knife comes in an individual plastic sheath.

BONING/UTILITY KNIFE $9.50
Excellent for boning chicken and other meats, and/or for general kitchen duties. Featuring a 103mm blade that curves to a point and a dishwasher-proof, black nylon handle, each knife comes in a plastic sheath.

SERRATED KNIFE $9.50
These knives are unbelievably useful. They are perfect for cutting cooked meats, ripe fruit and vegetables, and slicing bread and baking. Treated carefully, these blades stay sharp for years. The serrated 110mm blade is rounded at the end with a black (dishwasher-proof) nylon handle and each knife comes in an individual plastic sheath.

THREE-PIECE SET $20.00
This three-piece set includes a vegetable knife, a serrated knife (as described above) and a right-handed potato peeler with a matching black handle, presented in a white plastic wallet.

GIFT BOXED KNIFE SET $44.00
This set contains five knives plus a matching right-handed potato peeler. There is a straight bladed vegetable knife and a serrated knife (as above), as well as a handy 85mm serrated blade vegetable knife, a small (85mm) utility knife with a pointed tip and a smaller (85mm) serrated knife. These elegantly presented sets make ideal gifts.

SERRATED CARVING KNIFE $28.50
This fabulous knife cuts beautifully and is a pleasure to use, it's ideal for carving or cutting fresh bread. The 21cm serrated blade does not require sharpening. Once again the knife has a black moulded, dishwasher safe handle and comes in a plastic sheath.

STEEL $20.00
These steels have a 20cm 'blade' and measure 33cm in total. With its matching black handle the steel is an ideal companion to your own knives, or as a gift. Alison gets excellent results using these steels. N.B. Not for use with serrated knives.

PROBUS SPREADER/SCRAPER $6.50
After her knives, these are the most used tools in Alison's kitchen! With a comfortable plastic handle, metal shank and flexible plastic blade (suitable for use on non-stick surfaces), these are excellent for mixing muffin batters, stirring and scraping bowls, spreading icings, turning pikelets etc., etc....

NON-STICK TEFLON LINERS
These SureBrand Teflon liners are another essential kitchen item – they really help avoid the frustration of stuck-on baking, roasting or frying. Once you've used them, you'll wonder how you did without!

Round tin liner (for 15–23cm tins)	$6.50
Round tin liner (for 23–30cm tins)	$9.50
Square tin liner (for 15–23cm tins)	$6.50
Square tin liner (for 23–30cm tins)	$9.50
Ring tin liner (for 23cm tins)	$6.95
Baking sheet liner (33 × 44cm)	$13.95

Prices as at 1 November 2000, all prices **include** GST. Please add $3.50 post & packing to any knife/spreader order (any number of items), please note, Teflon prices include post & packing.

Make cheques payable to Alison Holst Mail Orders and post to:

Alison Holst Mail Orders
FREEPOST 124807
PO Box 17016
Wellington